'When you read her story of endurance and courage you realize how well-merited was the award to her of the DBE'

Manchester Evening News

'The author's disarmingly honest tales will make many old salts' hair stand on end'

Economist

'Absorbing reading – a feat of enormous physical endurance'

Morning Advertiser

'No addict of the salt-caked adventure will want to be without a copy of AT ONE WITH THE SEA'

The Bookseller

AT ONE WITH THE SEA

Naomi James

ARROW BOOKS

Arrow Books Ltd
3 Fitzroy Square, London W1P 6JD

An imprint of the Hutchinson Publishing Group

London Melbourne Sydney Auckland
Wellington Johannesburg and agencies
throughout the world

First published by Hutchinson/Stanley Paul 1979
Arrow edition 1980

Made and printed in Great Britain by
The Anchor Press Ltd, Tiptree, Essex

ISBN 0 09 921440 7

To Rob and Chay, my mentors

CONTENTS

ACKNOWLEDGEMENTS

This voyage depended on many people without whom its success would have been impossible. My deepest thanks go to Chay Blyth who lent me his yacht, and Quentin Wallop who financed the refitting. My sincere thanks also to the *Daily Express* for their backing of the venture. My food was all supplied by Philip Gerard-Jones and prepared by Claire Gerard-Jones and Maureen Blyth, who all gave so much – fondest gratitude.

Special thanks to Sailomat of Sweden and their terrific agent, Herman Brinks, for the excellent self-steering gear and for the trouble they went to throughout to ensure its continued serviceability. Many thanks also to Clifford and Snell for the loan of their emergency radio beacon and transmitter.

For photographic equipment I have to thank ITN, also for their interest and hard work and especially for financing the Azores rendezvous. Thanks also to Contax for supplying me with cameras and lenses.

Several local firms gave tremendous help in preparing the yacht before the start. I would especially like to mention Andrew Roberts of Dartmouth Yacht Services and his team, Trevor Read (masts) and Battarbee (hardware).

One of the most crucial problems was solved by the combined support of Quentin Wallop, my parents-in-law and Terry Bray, who underwrote the insurance for the yacht, without which I could not have sailed. Thanks also to the many firms who provided items of equipment free or at a welcome discount; particularly Grundig, International Paints, Racal, Lewmar, Spencers rigging, G. & M. Power Plant, Mountain Equipment

Ltd, Damart, and Ratsey and Lapthorn. My thanks to Southern Ocean Shipyard for checking over the yacht before departure.

On a more domestic note, my very special thanks and gratitude go to my sister Juliet and girlfriend Alexandra Akerman, who helped with so many things and kept me sane and organized throughout the last week before leaving.

My thanks are due also to the members of the Royal Cape Yacht Club who gave time and energy to help me refit in Cape Town in such a short time. I would especially like to thank Jerry Whitehead of Bootlicker, Douglas Binstead for the self-steering repairs, and the Alcocks and the Carters for their special help.

For the Hobart rendezvous I thank the *Hobart Mercury*, especially Malcolm Williams, and Bern Cuthbertson and his crew of the *Tasmanian Enterprise*.

Many Falkland Islanders gave me incredible help without which I'd never have been able to sail within three and a half days of arrival. Among them my very special thanks go to Les and Peggy Halladay, John Smith, Hilton Mathew, Willy Wilson and Ken Halladay. Also many thanks to the 'chippie' of the ice patrol ship *Endurance* for making the vital rigging parts. I should like to say a word of thanks to Alan Adair, the captain of HMS *Walkerton* for bringing his ship out to meet me. My thanks, too, to Roddy Bloomfield of Stanley Paul for all his help in editing this book.

Lastly, to the one without whom I could not have done it, my husband Rob, my love and thanks.

FOREWORD

by Chay Blyth

In this world there are people with good ideas and people with bad ideas. There are also people of action and people who just talk. The combination to beware of is the person of action who has the bad idea. Fortunately for us and for her Naomi James falls into the ideal category – the woman of action who has good ideas. She decided to become the first woman to sail alone around the world, hopefully non-stop, and once the decision was made there was no turning back.

I recognized this determination in Naomi when the subject of single-handed sailing was first broached. We were yarning and as so often happens the conversation turned to 'what is there left to do?' There is of course nothing original in the thought and I am sure a number of other women have mentally planned such a voyage, but to actually get down to details, to finding a boat and sponsors and supplies, is a very different matter. There are seemingly insuperable problems encountered at every turn, a dozen reasons why the whole project should be abandoned. Perhaps the biggest bogeys are lack of finance and lack of time and certainly these loomed large in Naomi's life.

On the day she met her husband-to-be Robert, Naomi started a courtship with the sea. Rob is one of the finest seamen I know and because he was skippering one or other of our yachts virtually all the year round he was able to teach Naomi first the rudiments and then the finesse of sailing.

Originally they planned to sail in the last Whitbread Round the World Race in *Great Britain II* but then a combination of circumstances – I will not spoil the book by revealing the fascinating story you are about to read – enabled Naomi to set out on her lonely sail. We loaned her our yacht *Spirit of Cutty Sark* which was renamed *Express Crusader*. I had bought her a couple of years previously and knew her to be a sturdy boat able to withstand the rigours of the Southern Oceans.

There were those who scoffed and shook their heads. Inevitably 'foolhardy' and 'no chance' were well-used phrases among the *doyens*. But then Chichester and Rose and others had been faced with the same comments and rightly regarded them as the least of their worries. Thankfully there were those who were quickly caught up in the sheer adventurous magnitude of it all and Naomi is first to credit the small army of people who gave help and encouragement to her. If a long lone sail is to be a success it must be preceded by dedicated teamwork and in this respect Naomi was more than fortunate. Friends, relatives, companies, enthusiasts – all gave time, energy, and advice. On 'down days' when depression really sets in, the weather is lousy and the yacht is taking one step forward and two steps back, I am sure it was the thought of her commitment to those back home that kept Naomi going.

The story that follows relates an epic sea voyage. It was not done for women's lib or to prove that anything man can do woman can do better. It was undertaken for that indefinable reason that makes men climb mountains and soar into the sky and fight the elements. It was achieved by a very special lady.

1
GREEN PASTURES

Wedged into a corner of the cockpit, muffled against the cold by thick oilskins, I watched intently as the light faded slowly from the sky. Lines of black rain squalls welled up over the horizon and passed low overhead, every now and then hitting *Crusader* with a savage blast of wind and rain. Somewhere behind that wall of cloud the sun was setting, and I searched the sky anxiously for a hint of colour — red or even the faintest touch of pink – which would tell me there wasn't going to be a storm tomorrow. Before the last storm the weather had looked the same as this but the sky had been copper, an ominous greenish-yellow colour which made my heart sink. Every night since then I had watched, staying on deck till my hands and face froze, knowing that *Crusader* probably couldn't stand another storm with her damaged mast, held up by my makeshift rigging. I still had to sail over a thousand miles to reach Cape Horn. The very thought of it sent a shiver down my spine. Another two weeks or more before I could reach the safety of the Falkland Islands . . . if ever. I no longer thought of getting there but simply of getting through each day as it came. More and more often I thought, what am I doing here? What on earth possessed me to come down to the lumpy, unfriendly and empty Southern Ocean. . . ?

My imagination had always been fired by other people's heroic feats, and when I day-dreamed as a child I was always a famous dancer or pianist or explorer, amazing people with my skill and daring. . . . In reality of course I was a timid, shy little girl, which was not surprising since I lived from birth to the age of twelve on a remote dairy farm with my brother, sisters and parents deep in the green pastures of Hawkes Bay, New Zealand. We seldom saw people apart from our two schoolteachers and when on the annual visit to the nearest town. Even then we children could scarcely be persuaded to leave the security of the car and face the frightening multitude of urban strangers who bore no relation to the friendly folk of our daydreams and bedtime stories.

Although we had such meagre contact with the outside world there were advantages in our life on the farm which more than made up for it. We had miles and miles of countryside to explore, and we could roam all day among the fields, rivers and scrublands suffering nothing more than torn clothes or scratched knees. Of the four children I, especially, liked to wander, and I frequently got lost. I think I inherited wanderlust from my father who was from one of the Irish Powers family and who had left County Waterford at the age of sixteen to find work in New Zealand. However, he had no connection with sailing so cannot be blamed for instilling into me a sympathy with the sea; indeed neither side of the family sported as much as a Sunday boat owner.– let alone an admiral or a captain. We were all very much landlubbers, and our major sporting interest was horse riding.

By the time we children were able to walk were also learning to ride – usually bareback and on hand-me-down ponies. Money was tight on the farm in those days, and we couldn't afford the sort of beast or equipment that belonged to some of our more affluent neighbours. But what we lacked in finery we made up for in tenacity, and there was scarcely a show or a hunt meet that didn't have a full contingent of Powers in evidence – not always doing the right thing but doing it with enthusiasm. There was no time for other sports, although we did once build a boat. Unfortunately, the building spot was half a mile from the nearest water – a duck pond – and by the time we had dragged this very large structure to the water's edge our interest in sailing had diminished; however, we launched the boat, but it promptly sank and all our remaining interest went with it.

Books were very important to us, and in the evenings reading was our favourite pastime. Both our parents are well read so there was always a wide selection of literature available. We 'lived' our books and the characters in them were real. They contrasted so much with the people of our small world that the extent of their attraction was immeasurable; neither could it be dulled by the influence of television as the goggle box hadn't yet arrived in New Zealand. Like all children we acted out these fictional or historical characters in our games. With no restraints from parents or environment these games became riotously uninhibited. Neighbours sometimes commented that we Powers kids behaved like wild Indians, but my mother would say that it didn't do any harm.

I can remember only one visit to the seaside while we were children, and on this occasion I got cramp from swimming too soon after eating. My brother Brendan also had to be hauled out of the water by his feet for similar impatience. I eventually taught myself to swim from a beach in Yugoslavia at the age of twenty-three.

Between the ages of five and twelve, I attended a tiny local school with my brother and two sisters. With childish guile and a sweet smile I was able to avoid doing any serious things such as sums and spelling and instead happily devoted my time to play and day-dreaming.

At the appropriate age my elder sisters Fiona and Juliet were sent to a Catholic boarding school. They missed the farm life very much and were miserable. I waited in trepidation for the same fate, but happily my parents moved to a larger farm in another district. Instead of boarding school I was sent to a local intermediate school where I received the shock of being put alone at a desk and expected to produce some work; twelve years old was late to start. Perhaps I never would have been much of a scholar, but now I found I could only apply myself to the subjects that interested me – and they weren't many. Although this move to the Bay of Plenty brought us more into contact with people, we still remained shy and spent our spare time at home.

When I was thirteen I was given my first horse – a hand-me-down from Juliet. She was newly broken in and as mean as a bucking bronc. Juliet had been thrown several times and, wisely, would have nothing more to do with her. I couldn't resist the chance of having a horse of my own, however nasty, and every day for a year we did battle. We soon established a working relationship; she would throw me and, having done so would let me ride her. I discovered within myself an obstinate streak. I'd made up my mind to ride her every day and realized that cowardice could be my only reason for giving up; stupidly enough, I cared about not being a coward.

I was a loner at school, had either one girlfriend or none and spent most of my spare time in the school library. I didn't like to be seen alone as it made me feel conspicuous, but I didn't seem to be able to make friends in a group.

I attended a girls' school in Rotorua. Fiona and Juliet were also there, but the school was so enormous I hardly ever saw them. As we progressed it was noted with mild astonishment that Fiona and Juliet were my sisters. The teachers obviously wondered how one family could produce such a variance of temperament and scholarly ability. I was bored and disinterested at school and spent almost the entire time day-dreaming. My reports got worse and worse and in exasperation Mother suggested that I should leave school and become apprenticed to the local hairdresser. I didn't care one way or another, but when the end of term exams came up and I was faced with the certainty of failing, I left and started a four and a half year apprenticeship.

When I reached my teens I spent more and more time by the stream on the farm, fishing or just staring at the ripples, and thinking. I loved being outside on wild stormy days when the wind shrieked through the trees and the water poured down the valleys in heavy rain. I was fascinated by the elements and fancied it was because they were uncontrolled by man: more likely I was suffering from an overdose of romantic literature.

Work suited me well. I'd always been a bit artistic and liked doing things with my hands. Being surrounded by women was of dubious merit, but it cured me of my provincial shyness and left me with a lasting dislike of tittle-tattle and gossip. I found I couldn't relate to the endless talk about homes, what the neighbours were up to, and what they were going to cook for dinner. There was much I wanted to learn about people, what made them tick and what made the world go round, but very few women that I met seemed interested in these subjects. I had to turn back to books and try to find out second-hand.

At seventeen I suddenly realized what an idiot I had been to leave school without a single qualification. I became self-conscious about my supposed stupidity and decided to try and rectify the situation. I went to night classes three times a week and at the end of a year passed 'O' levels in art and design.

The next year I took up German. My job had become boring and I decided I wanted to travel. Austria interested me because it epitomized the difference between the new culture of New Zealand and the old culture of Europe. Like most young people I went through stages of disliking the established order; my ex-classmates were marrying and producing, and I simply couldn't visualize myself doing the same. I wanted something different; what, I didn't know, but there had to be something else.

For the next three years until I was twenty-one I concentrated on saving for my proposed trip abroad. Juliet had also decided to go overseas, so we planned to travel together. I didn't go out much during this period and spent a lot of time at home building rock gardens.

When I wasn't moving heaps of rock I spent days on end riding. We had TV by now, but I didn't enjoy it much; evenings were for reading. I was marking time: there were many things I could have done, but having decided to leave I didn't want to become involved in anything that might tie me down. The future was a blank; I had the sensation that I would be stepping off into space, which was an interesting feeling. One thing I was quite sure of: I wanted to have control of my own future; I wanted to choose, not accept.

Juliet and I left New Zealand on New Year's Eve, 1970. We decided to start with a few months in England before braving a 'foreign' country. We went by ship which took nearly five weeks, and for the first three days of the voyage I was seasick – understandably so, I thought, as we went through the tail end of a cyclone. Once recovered I enjoyed life on board immensely; I learnt how to play chess and bridge, to enjoy Greek food and walk the many miles of swaying corridors and somehow end up at my pre-planned destination.

We arrived in England, took the boat-train to London and finally wound up in a flat in Richmond where we stayed for ten months. I got a job as a hairdresser but soon ditched it and tried my hand as a barmaid, fun though not very lucrative, but work took up comparatively little of my time or thinking; I was obsessed with more pressing and personal questions such as what I was going to do with my life. Working and living in London certainly wasn't the answer; I might just as well have stayed at home. On the ship Juliet and I made friends who came to live nearby, and for the first time in my life personal attraction completely upset my sense of independence and willpower – I felt incapable of resolving a thing for myself, a feeling I didn't like at all. I was dismayed to find I had no opinions of my own on any subject that mattered and was in danger of accepting those of my friends ad lib. I felt green and naive and became increasingly uneasy about expressing opinions which weren't mine and of which I wasn't convinced. At the end of ten months our small group began to scatter, and I decided to make the move to Austria I had always vaguely planned on.

Juliet had thought about going to Germany, but at the last minute didn't like the sound of the industrial town in which she was going to teach and instead came to Austria with me. We travelled to the mountain district of Tyrol where we hoped to work at a ski resort. Juliet couldn't speak German and I very little, so the chances of parleying our way into something sophisticated seemed very remote; we would have to be satisfied with anything. We finished up as waitresses which I hated, not least because there was never time to ski, which had been our main purpose for going there. After a month I took sick and when I recovered found the snow and the tourists had all disappeared. They didn't need waitresses in a snow-less, tourist-less ski resort, so we had to move on.

I went to stay with friends in France to recoup my health and make my next decisive move. With only £16 in my pocket I took the train to Vienna. It would be the first time in my life that I had been really alone – alone without my family or friends.

I got a job straight away in a hairdresser's – it seemed the only thing I could do as my German was very poor. But as soon as I began to understand the language sufficiently the old feelings of frustration returned: these people weren't only speaking another language, their attitudes and interests were foreign to me. Were gossip and other people's affairs the only things in the world that people talked about? Where were the people of my books, where was adventure, danger, some meaning to existence? It began to look as if I was in the wrong place to find them.

Until Juliet joined me six weeks later I scarcely spoke a word and certainly none of English. I was not surprised to find that after that time I was barely coherent. In the beginning it was a struggle being unable to speak the language, but I liked the feeling that being alone in a crowd gave me. I liked to feel myself apart from the people and their worries; in fact, I found that I preferred not knowing anyone. I tried to work out my reasons for this attitude and came to the conclusion that apart from my disillusionment with tittle-tattle, there must be an element of escapism. I couldn't relate to people very well, and I hated meeting them casually: I felt self-conscious and could never think of anything to say. I got into the habit of not looking at their faces as I walked down the street but instead stared into shop windows – much to the astonishment of Juliet who would see me walk straight past her.

I decided, however, that my state of anonymity couldn't last for ever, and I eventually set out to know a few people. I also took night classes in German at the university. As a result I discovered that I liked languages and wanted to speak German well.

In trying to find something I really wanted to do I also took classes in painting and clay modelling. Leisure hours I spent either reading in my room or walking the little streets and alleys of Vienna. I enjoyed listening to the strains of music which came from little courtyards hidden behind garden walls, or watching snowflakes drift past warm shop windows, shops that looked as though they'd been in existence for ever. I liked walking along the silent cobbled alleys where multitudes of carved figures and curious animals peered down from the tops of doorways and under the eaves.

I visited nearly every church in the city – a strange occupation for an atheist. Although the religious convictions of my childhood slowly dissolved over the years I liked churches and seldom passed one without a quick peep to see what it was like inside. The dark interiors were strange and haunting and stirred old memories of the days we used to go to a tiny old Maori church in a neighbouring village. The corners were lost in darkness, and I always wondered whether angels or devils were going to grow out of the walls.

I spent hours in Viennese cafés, watching little old ladies fervently dragging out their coffee and glass of water, playing out a ceremony I supposed they'd cherished for years. It gave me an odd feeling of desperation to imagine myself doing the same in years to come. Such morbid thoughts occupied my mind constantly and still I never got any closer to finding a solution. By the beginning of summer 1973 I'd had enough. I gave up my job and bought a bicycle. I found the best way of taking a close look at things was by walking, but, as carrying belongings on my back was obviously burdensome, I decided to buy a bicycle. However, I baulked at the thought of pedalling up all those Austrian mountains, so settled on a bike with a little engine on the back.

I left Vienna and headed off into the hills around the city. In a little saddle pack I had an extra pair of jeans and a sweater and some paperbacks. I chose the smallest roads I could find, so small some of them that occasionally I ended up in a farmer's back yard and had to back pedal in a hurry. The bike was super – it was light enough for me to pedal along the horizontal and had a strong enough engine to take me up the hills. After a few days on the flat I decided I was ready for the big stuff so I headed for the highest mountain pass in Austria, the Gross Glockner.

There was still snow on the mountains, and it was chilly; I raised a laugh and a cheer from motorists sitting in their steaming cars as I went pedalling by but right on the top I had to motor and pedal madly against the strong winds till I was over the brink and racing back to the warmth. The nights I spent in guest houses; after enduring one stay in a youth hostel filled with giggling, snoring German girls I had decided that peaceful nights were worth the price. The days were quiet and absorbing. I spoke to no one except when ordering a room and food, and I saw few cars. I managed to avoid the alarming characters I'd been warned about and, ten days after setting out, I crossed the German border and met up with some friends from Vienna. We loaded the bike into the back of their car and spent the next month in Switzerland.

By September I was in Greece. But I had already had enough of the idle, sun-drenched life and was pondering my next move. I'd run out of money but had vowed never to go back to hairdressing, so I had to think of something else to do. I'd been told about a school in London which held training courses in foreign language teaching, so I applied for an opening. My lack of qualifications might have deterred me, but I'd learnt that in Europe one can land quite surprising jobs if one bluffs through the preliminary stages. Unfortunately, the courses were booked up until February.

Back in Vienna I was getting very short of cash and on impulse I rang the directress of the Berlitz Language School where Juliet was working. I was invited for an interview, but before we could broach the dangerous subject of qualifications I explained that Juliet was my sister. It made all the difference.

They were fortunately very short of teachers too. By the end of a month of training I was teaching in front of a class only fractionally more frightened than I was. However, I got used to teaching adults more knowledgeable than myself, and when it became apparent that the student knew more about the subject than I, I would quickly change tack and start talking about idioms. Spelling was my weakest point and I studiously avoided writing anything on the blackboard.

My work was interesting, but I slowly came to realize that I'd never find what I wanted in a city. I now knew quite definitely the life I *didn't* want to lead, but I still had to find out what I *did* want. I decided to set off on my bike again.

In June 1975 I pedalled out of Vienna for the last time. It was a glorious feeling setting off into the blue with all ties cut and nothing to worry about. I loved covering ground and even if it was only fifty miles a day, I had a pleasant feeling of achievement.

While travelling along I let my thoughts range slowly, consciously giving myself plenty of time to decide where I was going and what I was going to do; I felt quite happy and sure I was right in challenging fate instead of waiting for something to turn up.

As the weeks spent cycling through Austria, Switzerland and then France went by I could feel a change slowly taking place within me. It was an uneventful way of life with nothing more exciting than having to dodge the occasional rain squall or hunting for a garage which would mend my bike. But it was an ideal antidote after four years in the city, and it enabled me to come to several realizations about myself: I liked the open-air life, I liked animals: therefore I decided I would go to England and look into the possibility of working with animals in a zoo, or even in a wild life park.

I wrote to my parents to tell them of my plans, sent my bike back to Juliet in Vienna, and headed for St Malo where I could catch the ferry and perhaps stop off at the Jersey Zoo en route. When I was looking for the ferry office a saucy young Frenchman, sensing I was lost, offered to show me the way.

As we walked together alone the quay a girl suddenly popped her head up from one of the moored yachts, by chance looking straight at us and asked: 'Anyone for coffee?' I laughed and walked on as she was clearly addressing the crew on her boat, but the Frenchman was equal to the occasion and replied, 'Yes, *two* please!' To my astonishment the girl insisted that we come on board, and I was introduced to the famous globe-circling yacht, *British Steel*.

The girl turned out to be a New Zealander travelling with her husband, and I was intrigued to hear that they were in a party which had chartered Chay Blyth's yacht and, with the skipper, had sailed across the Channel from England. I asked a lot of questions about the boat and Chay Blyth, both of whom I had vague recollections of hearing about in the past. I learnt that he had sailed *British Steel* round the world, alone and non-stop, the hard way from east to west against the favourable winds and currents. I found it difficult to believe. I wanted to hear more, and the girl suggested I come below to meet the skipper who she said was just coming alive after being up all night sailing. The Frenchman left, and I climbed down to meet Rob James.

2
THE TURNING POINT

Rob had sunbleached red hair, nice blue eyes and a very sun-burnt nose, and I liked him instantly. We chatted a while and he asked me if I'd like to join them for lunch – kippers and beans. I was enjoying myself and in no hurry to board the ferry, so I stayed and listened to some fascinating things. Rob talked to me about his sailing life, what he had done and what he planned for his future. We talked all the afternoon and into the night; wild horses wouldn't have dragged me away. Instead of finding a room for the night I slept in the boat's forward com-partment with one of the girls. By then I knew that for me everything had changed. At six in the morning Rob took *British Steel* out of the dock to sail for England, and I made my own way there by ferry, arranging to meet him again at Wey-mouth.

When I arrived off the ferry, Rob was there waiting for me. I had no definite plans so he invited me to join him at his parents' home in Andover and the following Sunday signed me on for *British Steel*'s next charter as deckhand/cook. It was an ambiti-ous title since I didn't know the front end of a boat from the back and, in addition, I couldn't cook.

On my first voyage I was paralytically seasick and could have cheerfully died, and on following occasions I wasn't much better. Learning the ropes was as confusing as learning a foreign language, and I'd never have stuck it if Rob hadn't been there. He allowed me to come on deck when it was rough and took over the cooking himself. I was astounded at Rob's patience in explaining the same things over and over again to each new charter crew and, of course, the repetition was very good tuition for me.

We sailed all week and spent the week-ends in Andover, and it was at this time that I got to know Chay Blyth and his wife, Maureen. I learnt that Chay was planning to enter *British Steel* in the Atlantic Triangle Race with a charter crew and Rob as skipper, which meant he would be away for six months. I badly wanted to go, too, but would have to pay my way – too much money for either of us to find or realistically borrow. Still, it was a good opportunity to go back to New Zealand and visit my family.

We finished the summer charters in the middle of September before the race and on 7 October I said a most upsetting good-bye. Everything seemed wrong about that day, and I dreaded the thought of the next six months without Rob. Furthermore I'd got used to doing what I wanted and I didn't like being thwarted in my desire to sail with him on this trip. However, I had to make the best of it and, anyway, going back to New Zealand to see my parents wasn't exactly a hardship; I had been away five years. After I'd had a few days to get used to the idea I was quite excited by the thought of visiting all my old haunts again and seeing my old dog, Taffy.

My father sent me over a ticket as I had virtually no money, and I arrived in Auckland five days after Rob's race started. My parents were there to meet me, and it was wonderful to see them.

During the six months in New Zealand I planned to earn money for my ticket back to England. Fortunately, the shearing season had just started and my brother Brendan offered me a job as 'fleeco' in his shearing gang. It meant throwing the fleece on to a table, sorting wool, sweeping the board etc. It was hard work rushing back and forth all day, but it required very little thought. I found the two-hour shifts rather long and tedious with nothing to look at or think about except the unappetizing bits of wool which covered me with wool grease.

To while away the time I drifted back into my old habit of day-dreaming. I thought about Rob and sailing and how good the future looked. Then I remembered an article I'd read in a magazine about a French girl who was going to try to sail round the world on her own. She was going to stop at various ports on the way and take three years to complete the trip. I tried to imagine what it would be like to sail for so long alone, and once I'd started thinking about it I began to fantasize. How would it be to say to myself, 'I sailed round the world alone'? I began to contemplate the possibility and after a while found the thought exciting although it also made me very nervous.

I decided to find out more. I had already read Chay Blyth's book, *The Impossible Voyage*, and from the library I borrowed books by all the well-known single-handed sailors: Sir Francis Chichester, Robin Knox-Johnson, David Lewis and half a dozen others. The more I read and the more I considered the details, the more the idea seemed feasible. But one thing that bothered me – in fact appalled me – was the thought of falling overboard. My skin crawled each time I thought of it. A picture would come into my mind of suddenly finding myself alone in the ocean with the boat sailing away from me. Those men must have been made of sterner stuff than me, if they had sailed on for months with that awful feeling in the backs of their minds.

I missed Rob very much, but I forced myself to be philosophical and remember the old cliché, 'absence makes the heart grow fonder'. Fortunately I had many interesting things to do at home which kept me busy. There was, for example, a young horse – only a foal when I had left five years earlier – who needed breaking in. This was a lengthy process but very rewarding for I was then able to ride him through all the canyons and the dirt tracks and the far corners of the farm.

There were very few people in Rotorua who I still knew, and I made no attempt to make any new friends as I was set on going back to England. I waited anxiously for news of Rob, but he could only write from the stopover ports of the race, Cape Town and Rio de Janeiro. When he eventually arrived in South Africa we sent each other telegrams, then letters, and from then on the waiting didn't seem so long.

I suspected my family were rather hoping that I might stay in New Zealand, but when the telegrams started going to and fro they must have realized that I had a very good reason for going back. I hadn't said much about Rob and nothing at all about my thoughts of sailing round the world. I didn't want to talk about plans I wasn't altogether sure about. I knew I wanted to spend the rest of my life with Rob, but we hadn't really talked about that yet; it would have to wait until the race was over.

It would also be the time to tell him about my still unresolved plan to sail alone around the world, although I knew instinctively that once the subject was broached I should be well and truly committed. It would be a commitment to myself alone, and if I were then to go back on the idea it would be a surrender I should find impossible to live with. What had begun in my childhood – little dares, like crossing a bridge from underneath by swinging along the supports, or riding a pony every day knowing she would throw me – had developed into a code of personal ethics which, like the staunchest religious devotee, I felt I had to follow, and failure to do so would make me lose faith in myself.

I had managed to scrape enough money together for my return fare (with a heavy loan from my ever-loving parents), and at the end of March 1976 I flew back to England. It was planned that I should stay with Rob's parents until *British Steel* arrived, although there was a rumour that she might have to call into the Azores for repairs, which would mean a few days' delay.

It was while staying in Andover and counting the days that I saw the answer to my fear of falling overboard. Rob's mother and I were travelling in a car when suddenly a cat ran out, the car braked and the seat belt tightened around me. I thought, *why couldn't something like that be adapted to a boat?* Yachtsmen do, of course, wear safety harnesses, and we had used them in rough weather on *British Steel*, but they are rather restrictive for ordinary use, and I didn't really want to wear one the whole time on my projected single-handed trip. If something like *this* could be used, something that would allow me free rein but would suddenly snatch tight if I were to fall, then it would be marvellous! (Later it was patiently explained to me that the principle of the car safety belt could never apply to a boat. But that was later; for the meantime, I had found the antidote to my one mental block, and it was at that moment that I finally made up my mind to try and sail single-handed around the world.)

At last, a week overdue, Rob got a radio telephone call through to say that they were sailing up the Channel, only a few miles from the finishing line at Gosport. Rob's father and I raced down to the Solent in the car and arrived just in time to see *British Steel* in the early morning light, spinnaker set, moving fast along the shore of the Solent. She was a glorious sight. Rob, I thought, looked even better when I saw him an hour later as they tied up alongside. He had a grin on his face which stretched from ear to ear, and when I later asked him why, he confessed that he'd completely forgotten what I looked like! Having been reminded he apologized for forgetting to take photos and suggested we get married immediately. I agreed!

Rob's parents were delighted and offered to see to all the arrangement as my parents were unable to come. We were married six weeks later at the end of May, and in true nautical spirit our friends and relatives sang, 'For those in peril on the sea' – very appropriate, I thought, as Rob had been stuck on the other side of the Channel the previous day on account of an imminent gale, while I imagined myself going through the marriage ceremony on my own. He made it, of course, and we spent part of our honeymoon in Plymouth looking at the boats about to depart on the OSTAR (*Observer* Single-handed Transatlantic Race).

While I had been in New Zealand, Chay had bought another yacht called *Spirit of Cutty Sark*; she was a well-known boat having been sailed in the 1968 OSTAR by Leslie Williams. Chay had her refitted and we used her on charter trips to France. I sailed in my usual capacity aboard this new boat and grew to like her enormously; little did I realize, however, the affection I was later to feel for her.

At sea again with Rob gave me the feeling that other people get from sitting together with intimate friends by the fireside. We were relaxed and completely at ease. One night while Rob was on the wheel I brought him a coffee and finally mentioned my idea. At first he was noncommittal but, after I'd discussed it with him a while, he realized that I'd already made up my mind. He thought I might not understand what I was letting myself in for, so I explained all the thinking I'd done in New Zealand and let him come to his own conclusions. It was very important to me that he had no reservations, because I wouldn't have made the attempt if he had been unhappy about it.

I needn't have worried; he thought it was a great idea, and, full of excitement, we started to plan how we would find a boat and a sponsor. The directors of Chay's company held a board meeting a few days later at which Rob brought up the subject of sponsorship. Chay and his agent, Terry Bond, had had much experience in that field and were very enthusiastic about the plan. They believed that finding a sponsor wouldn't pose too much of a problem, as it was the first attempt by a woman to sail round the world alone and non-stop. To add further interest I intended to leave England about two weeks before the fleet of yachts in the Whitbread Round the World Race. Their race was in four stages – stops in Cape Town, Auckland and Rio, and if I went non-stop I should be able to catch them up while they enjoyed a month in each port. I would then arrive back in England a few weeks after the main fleet. This appealed to me very much because instead of being left behind and worried, I would in a sense be with Rob, for he was taking part in the race as skipper of Chay's 77-foot ketch, *Great Britain II*.

But in spite of their optimism, no sponsor came forward during the next six months to take up our invitation. Nobody, it seemed, was willing to invest £60,000 (the amount needed to buy and refit a suitable boat) in a scheme involving a woman who'd never even once sailed single-handed before. I bought a couple of dazzling outfits to impress prospective sponsors in anticipation of some interviews; time was getting on and I hoped I might be able to get things on the move.

On Christmas Day, in Andover, we heard the news that *British Steel* with her reserve skipper had gone aground in the Canary Islands. Nobody had been hurt, but the loss – even the temporary loss – of the prize charter vessel would upset the entire summer programme. Chay decided to send out *Spirit of Cutty Sark* as a replacement. And so it was that in mid-winter, crossing the Bay of Biscay, I was to have my best heavy-weather experience yet when I accompanied Rob and his crew to Lanzarote. We left Dartmouth and had sailed a hundred miles before we had to turn back and run for shelter; I had never seen such appalling weather. Several days later we tried again and this time got as far as the French coast before we were forced to put into Cameret where we repaired the damages of a knockdown. It had happened as we were lying-a-hull in a force nine with all the sails down waiting for the weather to improve. A large breaking wave bowled us over; there were five of us on board and all of us, with the exception of Rob, ended up in the bilges along with the potatoes, onions, several bottles of cheap red wine and the engine which had broken from its mountings. There were a few bruises and a cracked rib, but the yacht herself was undamaged. I suffered dismally from seasickness, and as there was no respite in the weather I was unable to recover until we reached port. Across the Bay of Biscay we were forced back again and again; eventually we reached La Coruña in northern Spain, having given up trying to beat around Finisterre.

Here we decided to wait until there was a reasonable forecast. It was a long wait. One by one, our crew ran out of time and had to leave; eventually only Rob and myself remained. After three weeks of continual gales we set off with a force six to sail the remaining 900 miles to the Canary Islands. We had no self-steering gear and one of us had to do two hours on the helm while the other cooked, changed sail, slept, etc. Three days out, after a succession of gales and unable to hold down any food, I was exhausted and felt quite unable to take another turn at the wheel. Rob could see this so he ignored the ships, hove-to and together we had five hours' sleep. Then he cooked me a breakfast of bacon and egg and brought it to me in my bunk. After that I was better and gradually became used to the routine, but I was depressed at having become so exhausted and wondered how I should manage alone. Rob reminded me that I would have good self-steering equipment on my trip which would make things much easier, although he warned me never to allow myself to get so tired again.

We arrived in the Canaries in great spirits after nine days' sailing. We had only a month's charter, but Rob started to teach me navigation, and each day I took sun-sights and tried to plot our course from island to island.

I also did the navigation on the way back to England, although I was glad Rob was there, as I didn't altogether trust my ability to find land again.

On our arrival we had had news: all bids for sponsorship had failed, and the company had decided to sell *Spirit of Cutty Sark*. Apparently no one believed that I could sail round the world on my own, and many thought I would be foolish to try. I was bitterly disappointed, especially that *Cutty Sark* was being sold. I didn't mind so much that people were sceptical of my ability to make such a trip single-handed, but having to accept the fact that I couldn't go when I was so geared up for the voyage was a terrible blow. Rob and Chay tried to console me with the suggestion that I could go with Rob on *Great Britain II* in the Whitbread Round the World Race; I could even have the title of navigator!

I had to be content with that, but hadn't for one moment given up the idea of sailing round on my own. With such a race behind me I should be better able to convince people that I was capable of doing it again, alone. We now concentrated on getting *Great Britain II* ready. She had undergone a major refit in Dartmouth during the winter, but there were numerous things still to be done.

One evening, three weeks before the start of the race, Rob and I were invited to Chay's house next to the River Dart for a barbecue. It was here that I was introduced to a secret and very memorable cocktail called a 'yellow bird'. Not that it was the most memorable feature of the evening, but I'm sure it was the catalyst. After a superb meal, accompanied by the sound of crickets on the river bank, music, wine and more 'yellow birds', conversation took a serious turn when somebody asked me about sponsorship. One of *Great Britain II*'s crew, who had been a public relations man, heard the problem and to my amazement breezily announced that he personally could probably arrange sponsorship. The trouble was, he explained, that I had been setting my sights too high. If I could charter a boat like *Spirit of Cutty Sark* and content myself with just £10,000 for the preparation and fitting out, then I should be far more likely to attract sponsors. At this juncture Quentin Wallop, who himself owned a 75-foot cruising yacht, suddenly threw open his arms in an expansive gesture and said, 'I'll sponsor you for £10,000!'

I couldn't believe my ears and, judging by the silence, incredulity seemed to be general. A 'yellow bird' had got him.

But 'yellow birds' were pecking everyone that night for suddenly Chay looked up and, with matching gesture, added, 'Well, if you'll supply the cash, then I'll supply the boat. Naomi, you can take *Spirit of Cutty Sark*.'

I was speechless. They talked further about how much would be needed for the refit, and Rob told them we'd estimated the cost at a minimum of £10,000.

Then the question came up as to when I ought to go. The departure date I had always planned on was in about a week's time, but that was now obviously out of the question. Chay suggested that it would take at least a month to get all the equipment together and refit the yacht for single-handed sailing, so the earliest I could leave would be 3 September. Still, this would mean I should be rounding the Horn in about mid-March, which would be the end of the summer in that part of the world with still quite reasonable weather.

As I sat listening to all this my mind tried to absorb the facts. Everything had changed again; the plans I'd put aside and tried to forget for the moment suddenly took on the gigantic proportions of reality. The entire venture flashed before my eyes, giving me only a second to confirm in my mind that I really knew what I was doing. That second passed and I rejoined the discussion fully committed.

Above: Dressed up for a hunt meet — fourteen years ago

Top left: My first seafaring adventure

Left: Sixteen years old and already working

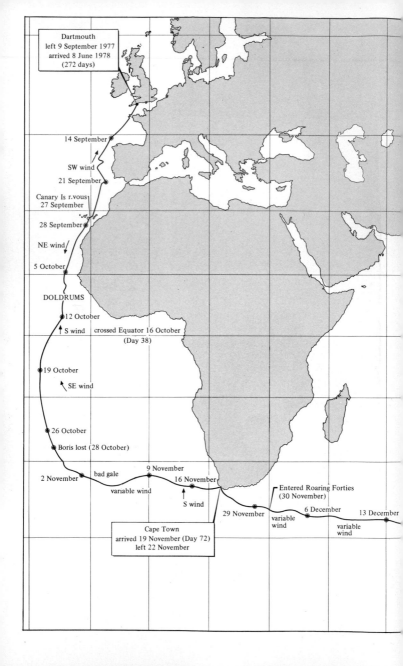

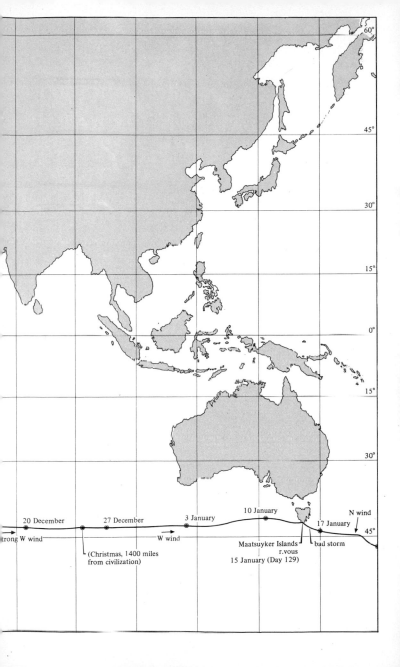

60°

45°

30°

15°

0°

15°

30°

20 December   27 December   3 January   10 January   N wind

trong W wind   W wind   17 January

                    (Christmas, 1400 miles   Maatsuyker Islands   bad storm
                    from civilization)   r.vous

                                                        15 January (Day 129)

45°

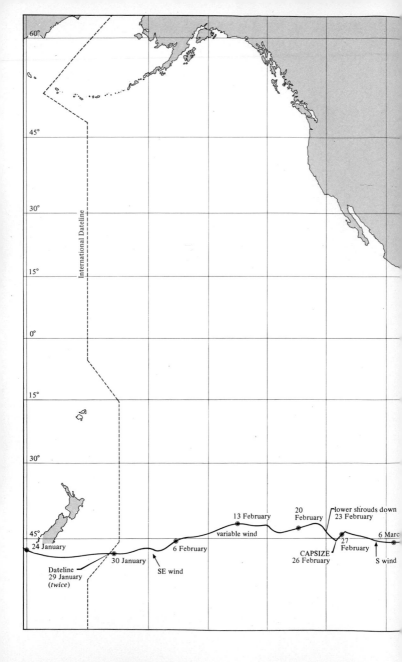

3 June

30 May

r.vous 24 May

SE wind

23 May

variable wind

16 May

9 May   NE wind

2 May
DOLDRUMS

met outward track,
28 April

25 April

SE wind

18 April

NW wind

11 April

variable wind

4 April

W wind

13 March

W wind

Falkland Islands
arrived 24 March
left 28 March

sighted land 21 March

19 March (Day 192) 70 miles south of Cape Horn

Above: Only a fraction of the food needed for one person for one year

Right: The strain of last-minute preparations shows on our faces

Above: Preparing sail shortly before departure

Left: Anything I can do to help?

Above: Sail handling is no problem in good weather

Right: Standing by for the noon-sight

Above: In the calm of the Doldrums Boris and I sunbathed on deck

Left: Boris takes an interest

Overleaf
Left: Hoisting the no. 2 genoa as I leave the Canaries rendezvous

Right: After eight weeks without seeing land Cape Town's Table Mountain was a sight never to be forgotten

Above: Cape Town well-wishers ensure that I don't suffer from thirst or lack of Dutch courage

Left: Resetting the Sailomat. (The success of the voyage depended largely on the Sailomat self-steering gear which did a remarkable job)

We all talked late into the night and then agreed to meet in the morning to examine the facts in the cold light of day. At home I must have asked Rob at least six times to remind me I wasn't dreaming. In the early hours of the morning I lay sleepless, realizing that through an incredible stroke of luck I had the chance to be the first woman to sail alone and non-stop around the world.

3
PREPARATIONS

It was now 3 August and we had exactly one month to prepare. In the morning a rather hollow-eyed Chay and Quentin arrived to outline the priorities. The important thing was to collect the vital pieces of equipment early, so without more ado Chay picked up the phone and ran his finger down the shopping list. The 'yellow birds' were having their revenge – every ten minutes he would groan and clutch his head. However, by the end of the morning he had ordered a new mainsail, eight self-tailing winches, an emergency radio, a foresail and anti-fouling paint for the hull. He was marvellous.

Rob had to spend most of his time on *Great Britain II* and from that day on could only help me in the evenings with phone calls and endless list-checking. It felt to me as if a bomb had been dropped on our lives; we were parting again. I was, however, far too busy to consider what the effects of further separation might be.

One problem that bothered us a lot was how to break the news to our families. The only member of my family I had told was Juliet, but I had asked her to keep quiet about it. She had been astounded at the time and had agreed that telling our parents wasn't going to be easy. Rob and I argued for days about who should ring his mother. His parents had been delighted about our marriage because they believed I would be a settling influence on him and he would live a less hectic life. Now his settling influence was off around the world on her own! Eventually he rang his mother and I wrote to my parents. The reaction was far better than we had anticipated. They had misgivings but seemed to understand my determination and, after the initial surprise and one or two puzzled outbursts, backed me one hundred per cent.

With both Rob and Chay leaving in a few days, I would have to see to most of the organization myself. We were very fortunate in having nearby a small firm called Dartmouth Yacht Services run by a quiet, efficient chap called Andrew Roberts who agreed to organize all the spares, to overhaul every object and fitting on the boat and to install the new equipment. He took a great deal of worry off my shoulders, although I was still fully occupied most of the time.

Initially, there were two major problems: a hold-up in hull and engine overhaul due to existing work at the local boatyard, and my inability to find a suitable self-steering gear. At the Southampton and London Boat Shows Rob and I had looked at all the available types but had been really interested in only one. It was a Swedish model called a Sailomat, new to the market and very sophisticated. It was expensive but for the sort of job it had to do the price was a small consideration. Chay had stressed that if my self-steering broke down less than three-quarters of the way round the world, I should have to call into the nearest port for repairs, and this would have defeated my objective to sail non-stop round the world. The trouble now was that it was holiday time and I could neither raise the agent in England nor get any reply from calls to the manufacturers in Sweden. Finally, in desperation I sent them telegrams and began to consider other types.

Every minute from now on was spent in some sort of preparation: making visits to the boat moored in the river; helping to remove instruments, winches and deck fittings, all of which had to be overhauled or replaced; sorting through sails and sending them to be repaired. Quentin took time off *Great Britain II* to chase up insurance, and Terry Bray, the PR man I met at the barbecue, enlisted the help of Lister Welch, an agent, who began to organize more sponsorship and helped me with innumerable small details.

A week had gone by and the pressure was really building up; although much had been arranged, the actual work on the boat had yet to begin. Insurance was another major problem, and I still hadn't heard from Sailomat in Sweden. I spent several hours on the phone each day, trying to keep tabs on various pieces of equipment and checking that items being made would be ready on time. I also had to squeeze in visits to the dentist to have crowns fitted (paradoxically one of the few places where I could relax)! My doctor next door promised to make up a suitable medical kit – which included inflatable splints. Everyone was remarkably helpful and I even got an overdraft from the bank!

Three days after Rob had left for the Fastnet Race I went home in the evening tired and depressed to find the long-awaited telegram from Sweden. I ripped it open and read, 'Sailomat available for immediate delivery'. I rang Sweden straight away and talked over the details of transport, costs etc. That was definitely one of the better days.

In just over a week all the vital pieces of equipment were in hand or on the way. I was being lent a radio telephone by Plessey's, and I'd even got my radio operator's licence.

Insurance was a real headache; Lloyds had refused to insure at any price. But the boat *had* to be insured. Chay had been incredibly generous to lend me his boat, but no one could expect him to risk losing £55,000! As with all my problems – insurance, electrics and engine – Chay was very sympathetic and reassured me that sailing around the world would feel like a doddle after the ordeal of getting things ready. I wished he wasn't going so soon, and I especially wished he could be there when I left. He was so matter-of-fact, and it was easy to get things done when Chay was around.

Rob and his crew arrived back unexpectedly! They had had to retire *Great Britain II* from the Fastnet Race due to long periods of calm which had threatened their planned preparation for the Whitbread Round the World Race and exhausted their stocks of food. Rob was able to help me considerably in the few days before his race began.

Meanwhile, buying my navigation equipment proved great fun. I had always wanted lots of nice things like sextants, parallel rulers, dividers etc. It made me feel very professional, although if anyone had asked me I'd have had to admit I wasn't exactly confident about using them. Rob had been a good teacher and kept the theory simple, but just in case I forgot anything vital I wrote it all down in my little book and put it in a safe place on board.

At the end of the second week I had a visit from Leslie Williams who had sailed *Spirit of Cutty Sark* in the 1968 Transatlantic Race. He was sailing in the Round the World Race in *Heath's Condor* and came aboard to see his old boat. He told me she was still his favourite boat, although that might have been partly because he had put a great deal of work into her. She was a glass-fibre production boat, designed by Van de Stadt and built by Tylers and Southern Ocean Shipyard. Considered to be a fast cruiser–racer in her time she had long been eclipsed by more radical designs. More important to me, however, was her comparison with Sir Francis Chichester's yacht *Gipsy Moth IV*. It was Chichester's overall time from England and back that I thought I had a chance of beating. It would be an ambitious challenge for – personalities, skills and experience apart – his boat had been specifically designed for the trip and single-handed sailing, while mine, of course, had not. Still, he had made a long stopover in Australia which I hoped would offset his advantage in boat speed.

I don't know what Leslie Williams made of all the obvious preparation and fitting-out work he saw as he nosed affectionately around his old boat, but if he had any intimation of my one-woman attempt he kept discreetly quiet. I was keeping the plan a secret until ten days before departure as I didn't want any other woman beating me to it!

With Rob away working on *Great Britain II* at Hamble I mostly worked late into the evenings and started to appreciate television as a way of relaxing.

One evening I was in the middle of making out food lists and thinking of the daunting prospect of getting it all together when I was contacted by a friend, Philip Gerard-Jones, a baker from Wales. He was supplying *Great Britain II* with bread and cakes and wanted to know if I would like some. He also suggested I send him my food lists the next morning. A few days later he rang to say he would provide everything on the lists and a few more items besides! I didn't know how to thank him.

Several days later, in the pouring rain, Philip arrived with his wife, Claire, their two children, a dog and about a ton of tinned and dehydrated food. They deposited it all in the lounge and had a cup of tea before starting back for Wales. When I tried to thank them they said, 'Oh, it's nothing, we're enjoying it.' Claire had written out detailed lists of the quantities and the many items they'd added – some quite basic things which I'd forgotten, like biscuits and sweets. She also supplied me with a copy of a Cunard menu in case I needed ideas in the galley.

I was very grateful to them for their thoughtfulness and all the trouble they'd taken. The tinned food, however, had to be specially prepared for the voyage, and Maureen Blyth offered to do this – a job she'd done for Chay three times already. All the tins had to have their labels removed, then be varnished and relabelled with paint or indelible ink; if this wasn't done the tins rusted and the paper labels disappeared, so one never knew whether to expect a lamb stew or creamed rice pudding. It was a tedious, smelly job that Maureen must have hated – how she ever found the time in her busy life I couldn't imagine, but often I came home late and found her there, varnishing tins, and sometimes even in the early morning before I'd left. For days the house looked and smelled like a hardware shop in the process of demolition.

By the end of the second week I was making more phone calls than a full-time operator, and I was not altogether surprised when I woke one morning to find I had lost my voice. This was serious because I had a call arranged to Sweden in the afternoon to enquire about my Sailomat self-steering. I rushed to the chemist's and spent lunch bent over a steaming potion which stung my eyes and tickled my nose but bypassed the problem altogether. I didn't have a cold and didn't feel ill, so had to assume I'd been talking too much. The remedy was to shut up for a while, so I whispered for the rest of the day and was just able to make myself understood to the Sailomat people, though they must have thought I sounded very strange.

By keeping conversation to a minimum for the next few days I recovered my voice in time to be able to talk to Rob when I visited him at Hamble. We spent the night with his parents in Andover and had a quiet, relaxing evening with a family who could talk about other things besides boats.

In the morning I dropped Rob at *Great Britain II* and visited Plessey's factory nearby to talk about the promised radio. Unfortunately, the model I was hoping to borrow, designed for the army, was not approved for commercial use by the Post Office, which was to pose some serious problems. Very worried, I drove to Hamble to talk to Rob, who suggested I buy a more conventional type. This might be possible as my new agent had found some additional sponsorship which included the *Daily Express*; its editor, Derek Jameson, didn't seem to think it at all unusual that a woman should want to sail round the world on her own. It was now 19 August, two weeks before the proposed departure.

I had been given a kitten to take with me for company. I was uncertain of his merits as a companion as I'm not very fond of cats, but I thought with his sharper senses he might serve very usefully as a 'radar' – meowing or reacting in some other way when a ship or some unfamiliar object came very near. He was, however, a rather pocket-sized radar, no more than five inches long, fluffy and still very attached to his mum. I decided not to take him aboard until the last minute so that he would have a chance to grow up a bit first.

On the 22nd I went to Portsmouth where I spent a night with Rob and visited some of the other yachts in the race. I also joined in a pre-race party in which the crew really let their hair down – probably thinking of the weeks they would spend in close confinement and (almost) total abstinence.

The next day I went to London to see Derek Jameson of the *Daily Express*. The sponsorship entailed filming and writing articles which would be collected at prearranged rendezvous plus sending short radio reports every week or so. The sponsors were also paying to have the name of the yacht changed to *Express Crusader* – a crusader is the motif which appears under the newspaper's banner.

Thankful that some of the worst problems were sorting themselves out, I drove wearily to Andover where Rob and I were to
spend our last night together. In the morning I dropped him at
Portsmouth and we said good-bye. We were both so reconciled
to the situation that neither of us were very emotional – my
thoughts and feelings had for some time been totally involved
with the forthcoming voyage; Rob knew this and responded in
his own way. The fact that we would now be physically apart
didn't disturb us unduly at the time. In a way we had made a
sort of parting the day my trip became a reality. I had to reduce
my dependence on him and constantly remind myself that for
nine months I'd have to rely on myself entirely.

So much had had to change on that day. At times I felt I'd
given myself a death sentence, but still the thought of changing
my mind was impossible.

I called into the boatyard on the way back to Dartmouth and
found the boat out of the water. The men from Phillips boatyard were working on the engine but were unable to get certain
replacement parts. They said the boat couldn't be relaunched
until Tuesday, only four days before the departure date which I
was desperately insisting upon. I had been insistent because I
felt the more time they believed they had for the job the longer
it would take. The weather, however, was an important concern
for not wanting any delay; even a few days could mean an
entirely different weather pattern around the Horn.

Meanwhile, the Sailomat arrived and so did the boat builder's
representative. He spent several hours looking over the boat
and, apart from work on a couple of welds which was completed
the next day, he pronounced her sound, which was very comforting. With only a week or so to go she looked a frightful mess.

I rang Racal Communications who had supplied *Great
Britain II* with a radio and asked them if they had a set available.
They said that they had and could deliver, install and fit new
crystals by Saturday – and it would cost me £4500! I felt quite
faint. Fortunately, they were prepared to make a considerable
reduction, and I ended up with a very powerful radio which I
knew would keep me in contact with Rob at certain important
points of the voyage.

Insurance was a continuing problem. On no account could I go without it, and yet it seemed impossible to get. In the dark corners of my mind there lurked the unpalatable knowledge that, if it was the only alternative, I would sneak off in the dead of night. If Chay had been in the same situation I'm not sure what he would have done. Fortunately the problem was solved by my parents-in-law, Quentin and Terry Bray, who between them underwrote the yacht to the value of £50,000 – an incredible gesture of confidence.

Maureen invited me for dinner the day Rob's race started. I knew I should stay by the phone but couldn't resist the idea of relaxing. I tried to imagine what Rob would be doing now the race was under way. I hoped they'd had a good start. When I arrived home I found his telegram: 'Good luck, may see you at the Horn', it said. Then Rob's father rang to say that Rob had called, full of jubilation, having got the best start and that he was holding on to the lead. He had tried to call me, too; I felt terribly disappointed.

The next few days were hectic. I scrubbed the hull with an abrasive cleaner and a pot scourer, and the boat was put back into the water for the mast to be stepped. The day before, a crack had been discovered in the forestay-fitting at the top of the mast. It meant a day's delay rewelding, but it was not the sort of thing that could be left to chance. I could just imagine myself in a few months' time, worried silly about a fault up the mast and wincing every time the wind blew.

Each evening during the final week I relaxed for half an hour in a luxurious hot bath. I tried to reason that I wouldn't have this pleasure for the next nine months – but I couldn't make myself appreciate what I would later be missing.

Apart from my bathtime, the last few days were ringed with incredible chaos. Juliet, my sister, and a friend, Alexandra, arrived to help me organize things. I had put all the suitable clothes I planned to take in heaps on the floor, and they sorted them into changes and sealed them in polythene bags. All the perishable food such as sugar, cereal etc. they repacked into smaller quantities and sealed; they then organized the food which Philip had delivered, so that it could be taken aboard as soon as the interior had been cleared of workmen's tools.

The 2nd of September and the eve of my proposed departure was the day to crown all horrible days. I went down to the boat and discovered some pieces of vital equipment still hadn't arrived. To make matters worse Andrew hadn't yet been able to check the sea-cocks or the hoses which connected the fuel lines from the tank to the engine. He suggested that I delay the departure. I knew he wanted everything to be in perfect working order, and that he wouldn't let me go anyway till he was satisfied, so I agreed to leave on Wednesday, the 7th.

The Sailomat self-steering was fitted and the company sent their agent to show me how to use it. We went a few miles out to sea and there was a nice breeze which blew away the cobwebs of uncertainty which had been building up over the weeks and days. The self-steering gear worked perfectly.

Now things began to go smoothly; the boat was cleaned up, and we started to load the food. Andrew and his team worked like beavers renewing rusty or dubious-looking fittings and fixing new fuel lines. It had been explained to me in great detail what I should do if the engine failed, and there was an impressive array of spare parts in the cabin workshop, but I viewed them with dismay as I really hadn't the faintest idea where they fitted.

Rob called a few times and was delighted to hear I'd be on my way soon. On the 6th we finished loading the food, but the girls stayed working on the boat till two in the morning. They insisted I go home and try to sleep and, reluctantly, I obeyed.

I didn't sleep very well – my head was still buzzing with the echo of a hundred phone calls, and I had a knot of anxiety in my stomach. I tried not to think of the next day but went through countless lists in my head, wondering whether I'd forgotten anything vital. At last I fell into a fitful sleep and had strange disconnected dreams which I later tried to analyse. My dreams have always been prolific and vivid and often closely connected with what I'm doing at the time, and if what I'm doing is wrong for me, my dreams invariably tell me. There was nothing disturbing about them that night so I was glad that my subconscious approved of what the rest of me was up to.

After breakfast I left the house for the last time, gathering up a big pile of telegrams on the way out. They were pouring in now from all over the place: one from Chay read, 'Only three turns left, then one right and home sweet home'!

A lot of people had gathered on the quay to watch and comment on what was going on. Over the days the helpers working on the boat had been amused by the speculations of the interested public. I was usually too busy to take any notice of what they said and, anyway, if they thought I was mad, so what? I wasn't going to argue the point with them.

I'd decided to leave at mid-day so, with a few hours still to spare, Andrew, myself, Juliet and Alexandra, and a crew of workers motored up to the fuel berth to top up the water and fuel, and horrors – the engine stopped. Andrew disappeared into the bilges and emerged looking grim. The fuel pump was faulty, and it was imperative to get a new one. Dazed at this new setback we got a tow to the mooring and Andrew set about getting a new pump. An hour later he told me it would take till the night of the 8th to procure and install. There was nothing to do but accept the situation and make use of the delay. I found more cassettes and books, and whiled away the rest of the time impatiently. By the morning of the 9th all was set to go again. After taking on more water and fuel we returned to the quay to sort out the sheets and sails and stow the last items of gear. Then Andrew, Alexandra and helpers hoisted the sails and connected the self-steering gear, and we slowly moved out to the entrance of the river. The Royal Dart Yacht Club had kindly offered to fire a gun across the starting line, and we delayed a few minutes before reaching the line to finish a last repair. Then friends and helpers all said their good-byes and got into a launch. Juliet had already sneaked off to frustrate the photographers who would have loved to film an emotional parting – she had waved good-bye from the quay earlier in the morning and I was the only one who noticed her leave. I suddenly heard a gun crack and realized I was across the line and had started my 30,000-mile journey.

4

CRUSADER UNDER WAY

9th September (Day 1)

When the launch turned for home and I had waved my last good-bye I looked around for some work and discovered there was nothing to do! The sails were up and setting, *Crusader* was pointing more or less in the right direction, and the Sailomat was controlling the course. The contrast between having had more to do than I could reasonably cope with during the preparations, and now finding myself with empty hands was so marked that I abruptly sat down in the cockpit and stared at the coast as it rapidly grew smaller astern. A few yachts still accompanied me but *Crusader* was moving well and leaving them behind. I had time now to wonder at the self-steering gear and to see what a valuable piece of equipment it was. I thought abstractedly of the Sailomat going on twenty-four hours a day without getting tired – provided it didn't break. If it did break I would have to spend all my time at the helm until I could reach a port for repairs. I was reminded of Chay's glum pronouncement to this effect. But here I was, a mile from Dartmouth and thinking about having to turn back already!

I jumped up, pumped up some water for a cup of tea and thought about the navigation. It was nice and calm with a steady fifteen-knot wind, but blowing from Ushant which was the direction in which I wanted to go. So, instead of being able to steer for the exit of the English Channel and thence into the Bay of Biscay, here I was blithely steering towards the Channel Islands. However, I reflected that my boat was able to steer closer into the wind than many an older boat, and that even if

the wind didn't shift I knew my zigzag course would get me
there eventually. Having plotted my course I re-read the telegram I had received that morning from Rob.

> Work out approximate courses before leaving. Get help with
> new sails before start. Under-canvas if in doubt. Take it slow
> and steady. Think out problems. Ask advice via *Express* if
> necessary. Leave any messages with Father. Good Luck.
> Love Rob.

He wasn't leaving anything to chance!

I hung the cable in front of the chart table to remind myself
that Rob wasn't really very far away, and was concerned. I
supposed that he'd be well past the Canaries by now, about
1400 miles from me and probably out of radio range.

I jumped on deck again to make sure there were no ships
sneaking up on me and had another look at England. It was
hazy and the coast showed only as a blurred outline; one or two
ships were visible but they were a long way off. I was suddenly
acutely aware of space and a huge feeling of relief. I could do
whatever I liked from this moment on with nobody to see my
mistakes. I could take my time! All I had to do was to point the
yacht in the right direction and make sure I didn't run into any
rocks or boats. Easy! Feeling remarkably content I went down
below and made a cup of tea.

My kitten, named Boris, didn't want anything to eat, and
didn't look very well. He kept staring in fascination at the
flexible fuel tank lying on the quarter berth wobbling like a
water bed. I drank my tea and got out the glue to stick down a
corner of roof lining that was annoying me.

Towards evening (Day 1) I wrote in my log:

> I'm feeling seasick which tends to make things appear rather
> grey, although Boris, I see, after being sick is eating like a
> horse, so I should be thankful for small mercies. I've done all
> I can to make myself happy with the navigation and fixed my
> position with the various landmarks; now that it's getting
> dark I've turned the masthead- and side-lights on. There are
> quite a few ships about. I tried calling Rob on our pre-

arranged schedule but couldn't raise him. I must be well out of range so I'll have to be content to hear things second-hand from his father.

And, later still I wrote:

Finally sick and now I feel better. There are times when being sick is the only way to get relief. It's 11.30 p.m. and I'm watching a ship go slowly by. Sometimes these monsters take ages. I'm sleeping as best I can, but setting my alarm clock to ring at twenty-minute intervals.

Twenty minutes is the average time they reckon it can take a ship to come from over the horizon to hit you. Some ships, I suppose, take longer, while there must be other ships which can close the gap in far *less* time. Still, one cannot keep awake every minute of the day and night and I reckoned that it would have to be an awfully mean ship to sneak up on me while I was having a little snooze! There has to be a certain amount of luck involved, of course, and I tried to calculate by my special law of averages the chances of being run down. Let's say there is about a fifty-fifty chance that the ship on the horizon is on a collision course, then another fifty-fifty chance that the watch-keeper on that ship is not looking out, then there is the much smaller chance that it is approaching when I'm not looking. . . . All in all, I decided that the chances of being run down while keeping a reasonable watch calculated were fairly slim. Later, during the night, there was an incident to disprove my theory.

I saw a ship approaching and thought it would clear quite easily without my altering course, but I stayed on deck to watch. When it was only about a quarter of a mile away it suddenly seemed to alter course and head straight across my bows. Perhaps I was half asleep, but I realized with a jolt that it was going to pass much too close. Actually, the vessel was supposed to give way to me, but I wasn't going to hang around to argue the point. I swung the wheel hard over and went under its stern. It was a shock to see a massive steel wall plough past, ablaze with lights. As I wallowed in his wake, I flashed my torch at the boat furiously, wishing I could signal something nasty, but my knowledge of Morse only stretches to SOS and, anyway, it was obvious – no one was keeping watch.

I was dismayed at my slow reactions over this incident; I was already quite tired, and it was only the first night. I could expect heavy shipping for the next few days and then there would be fishing boats. In the early hours of the morning, I sailed straight into a fleet of them. There were dozens all round, and I stayed up to make sure I didn't run into any of them. Fishing boats are rather awkward things: they are apt to go round in circles. Just when you think you've been clever and found a clear path, you'll find they're heading straight at you again! To my relief these seemed to keep a very good watch and never came too close. Nevertheless, I was glad when at last I left them behind and I could go below to make myself a hot drink.

My dinner during the night had been some water biscuits and four chocolates; I'd managed about four fifteen-minute snoozes. I had had to change tack in the night to get on course for Ushant but the Sailomat made this considerably easier, for I had only to adjust the angle of the wind vane to suit the next heading and the boat automatically came around to its new course, leaving me free to do the job of winching in the foresail.

I was feeling quite jaded, but it was daylight again which made everything look much more cheerful, and at least I'd come through the night in one piece. I looked at my fluffy 'radar set' sleeping blissfully on my bunk and decided to give him another chance. After all, it had been his first night, too.

There was no sight of land in the morning; this was as it should have been, although the visibility had been so good in the night that I'd seen the lights marking some of the Channel Island hazards. Towards mid-morning I took a sun-sight and another at mid-day, and when I'd plotted them was surprised to find that I was much further ahead than estimated. Then I looked out of the hatch and saw the coast of France bright and clear! I spotted the big water tower north-east of Ushant and identified it on the chart. So far so good.

I could see that I wasn't going to clear the headland on my

present tack, so I headed away from the coast for a while which gave me an opportunity to try the radio. The radio had all sorts of frequencies and megacycles which were a mystery to me, but I'd been shown how it worked and assured operation was simple. I switched on and called Portishead, the main long-distance radio station. Nobody answered. I fiddled about with the knobs and when I tried 2182 megacycles, the international distress frequency, I heard someone talking to a coast station. As soon as they'd finished speaking I asked if anyone could hear me, and immediately a man's voice replied, asking me which of the various working frequencies I'd care to use. I had none of those he mentioned, so explained that I really wanted to talk to Portishead. He kindly put me through.

I felt silly and incompetent, but they were friendly and cheerfully connected me with Rob's father. He said the boat had looked super on the television news! I gave my position, told him all was well and signed off, as I was worried about some ships close by.

I knew this stretch of France fairly well, having sailed here with Rob, and I remembered the strong tides, so I took good care to check them in the almanac. As I approached Ushant the tide was against me, and the wind, still dead ahead, was dying. For ages I tacked back and forth and seemed to get nowhere, but I knew the tide would turn at mid-afternoon and then, hopefully, I would be carried past it.

Towards nightfall I was still trying to pass Ushant – that wretched piece of land! The beam from the lighthouse was starting to flash across the sails; the wind had almost disappeared and I was nervous about being too close when the tide turned again. I put about and headed out to sea and held that course all night. I was still keeping the same twenty-minute watch system but sleeping better now, probably because I was so tired. Once I had to sit up for an hour and a half, glaring balefully at a trawler which would persist in making friendly passes in my direction. No sooner had he pushed off than several large tankers went thumping by, disturbing the quiet night with their engines. I began to dislike ships intensely when they came within my range, although I had previously imagined that their size and stability, and the fact that there was life aboard them, would offer some comfort.

By midnight I was thoroughly fed up and wrote in my log:

> The trouble with Tilley lamps is they make so much noise! And what a performance to light! I thought I should try using the lamp instead of the electric lights to save the batteries, but what a nasty hissing noise the Tilley lamp makes. I haven't figured out yet if I can re-use a mantle. If not, then I have only enough of them for about twenty-four nights; I'll save the lamp for the Roaring Forties.

The night seemed endless and by the time day broke, with no land in sight, I suspected I'd drifted back past Ushant. The wind had only come in fits and starts, and I'd had trouble working out my position from the lights on shore, none of which appeared to match the ones on my chart. However, I was without doubt in the Bay of Biscay. A big swell was running and making things uncomfortable down below.

I managed a sun-sight in the early morning and, although it was just a glimpse through the clouds, it put my position thirty miles past Ushant, and I was happy to accept that! However, my noon-sight later showed it was likely to be incorrect, and I worried about where I had made the mistake. I took two more sights but wasn't happy with either. Then I took a further two at about 4 p.m. which suggested that I wasn't as far ahead as the others had put me. It was all rather confusing. The meandering in the night had played havoc with my dead-reckoning position, and I thought it might help if I watched the passing ships, hoping they were keeping to their prescribed traffic lanes which were more or less in the direction I was going.

I slept for one and a half hours in the afternoon after clearing some wood shavings from the cockpit. I noted in my log:

> I don't feel too bad now, propped up here by the chart table, tired but not exhausted. The motion of the boat is steady and I'm getting used to it, in fact this is the fastest recovery from seasickness I've ever made. Boris is playing out of sight in the

saloon, I can hear the occasional scratch and spit. He's just had a big feed of my goulash which he enjoyed. He's a dear little thing, quite affectionate at times and throughly able to amuse himself.

12th September (Day 4)
The wind has gone round and is blowing me along at six to seven knots. The seas are big and make the boat roll heavily at times, which in turn takes the wind out of the sails. This makes them slat and the blocks bang and clank, so all in all it's rather noisy. The sun is trying to shine through blotchy layers of cloud, and I'm hoping it will come out at 12.30 when I must take the noon-sight. Then I'll discover where I am – I hope! I took two sights this morning and although they put me approximately where I thought I was, they varied from each other by twelve miles, which shows that I haven't perfected the art. With practice I expect I'll become more accurate.

The first half of the night was disturbed by the frequent ringing of the off-course alarm. *Crusader* had been unable to hold her proper heading in the fickle winds and by midnight the wind had dropped completely. She rolled aimlessly for an hour until the wind got up from the north-west and I was able to set a compass course of 220°. I was also keeping a close lookout for ships, because according to the chart I'd be crossing a shipping lane about midnight. Thereafter I slept soundly until 7 a.m. when I awoke with a fright and bolted on deck to find it was daylight. *Crusader* was sailing along happily, but the wind had veered a little and she was slightly off course. I ran off and eased the sails. The Sailomat didn't like the wind almost dead astern, so I altered course a little to bring the wind on the quarter. I was concerned at a grating noise coming from the self-steering and found one of the mounting bolts loose; fortunately the noise stopped when I tightened the bolt.

I found that I wasn't at all bothered by seasickness now, even in the galley. For breakfast I fried leftovers of potatoes and peas with two fried eggs and had to fend off the cat while I ate. Eventually I gave him some, but he was more interested in climbing on to my plate. He certainly had some perverse habits – sleeping during the day and playing at night, and sitting on the charts when I was trying to navigate.

In the afternoon I noted:

> My loo has packed up. Probably the one thing that wasn't overhauled as it was a non-vital piece of equipment! Now like other single-handers I've taken up with the good old bucket – one of my shiny new ones, it seems such a shame. One day when I'm feeling particularly brave I'll tackle the loo and see if I can find the cause of the breakdown, although that's going to have to be a *very* good day!

In the late afternoon I attempted my first really arduous piece of sail handling which made me acutely aware of the limits of my physical strength. When the wind is dead astern the boat goes faster if the sails can be 'boomed out' on each side. Unfortunately – in the case of the foresail – this means having to balance on the rolling foredeck manoeuvring a long and heavy pole. It is difficult because the pole has to be held up a few feet at the outboard end by a halyard, while the other end has to be lifted and fitted to the mast. If I were to choose the wrong moment, when the boat is rolling awkwardly, then there would be a very real danger of losing control of the pole and following it over the side. I was a very careful beginner and took nearly one and a half hours to complete this simple operation of 'goose-winging', but it was worth it; the boat's speed jumped to over eight knots and held it for a considerable number of hours.

I felt quite worn out and headachey when I had finished and went below to cook something hot in case action was called for in the night. When I'd eaten I called up Portishead Radio who had a telegram for me from Rob. 'Well done, good luck, thinking of you all the time, love Rob.'

Dear Rob! There had been so much to think about in the past few days that I had only had odd moments to concentrate on him. In truth I had deliberately blocked him out of my mind, for all my energies and thoughts had to be directed to the present; the past had already become dim and unreal. This reminder in the form of a telegram suddenly put Rob in a different perspective for me. He wasn't behind, he was in front, not just physically but in a tangible, comforting way and from then on he seemed quite near and returned to my thoughts in the old way.

I went to bed as soon as it was dark, partly to save lights and partly because I was very tired. I was out of the shipping lanes but occasionally still saw ships, so I kept on the masthead light and reduced my watches to an hour. It wasn't really an efficient lookout but I thought, illogically I admit, that as I'd almost been hit once, I was probably all right for a while. I had come to hate the sound of the alarm clock and as a defence would waken myself just before it went off. However, I never trusted myself to wake without it.

The sound of the alarm clock was bad enough, but the off-course alarm was worse. It had evil connotations: it not only meant a change of wind direction but the probability of an increase or decrease of wind as well. This, in turn, might mean having to stay up on deck and change sails, and that was an unpleasant prospect in the middle of the night. When the alarm clock went off, however, I would just jump up on deck, take a quick look round and dive back into my sleeping bag again.

Although I cursed it, the off-course alarm allowed me to keep up a good constant course. It was electronic device with a long and irritating buzz which one simply couldn't ignore. If the wind was flukey the buzzer seemed to go half the night, and in the first week I seldom had more than an hour's sleep at a time. But I must have been getting used to these odd hours because I felt quite well, and I didn't need to sleep during the day. However, when I changed sails I noticed that I tired very quickly, and so I tackled each job to work slowly and carefully. I also remembered Chay's constant warnings about hot food and made myself cook at least one hot brew a day, sometimes three!

I spent the entire fifth morning handling sails. The wind went round so I had to take the pole down and gybe. I wasn't very happy with the way I handled the operation. As the boat's stern went through the wind the mainsail and boom flew across to the other side so violently that there was a terrific crack. I decided I should have to figure out a more careful procedure for gybing or I would probably break the mast! After lunch I noticed the wind speed was increasing with each successive roll. The wind indicator said twenty-five knots, and that was already too much for a full mainsail. It was time to put in a reef. It was the first time I'd tried to reduce the mainsail area on my own, and when I'd finished I had to admit it wasn't the best reefed main I'd ever seen, but nevertheless not bad for an amateur. There were a few tufts of canvas and the odd wrinkle, but there wasn't time to ponder: the wind was increasing still further, so I left the mainsail and took down the big foresail – the No. 1 yankee. I preferred the yankees to the slightly larger genoas because they were higher cut and therefore easier to lower and get inboard. I changed the No. 1 for the No. 2 yankee, which also took me a while as I couldn't decide on the right length of strop to put on the head of the sail, and in the end chose the wrong one and had to change it. Lowering sails was another skill ripe for improvement. For the moment, in any amount of wind, I was simply letting go the halyard and allowing them to drop into the water. It didn't appear to damage them and it was much easier to drag a wet sail aboard than use the alternative method of hanging on to the halyard for a controlled descent and then fighting with the flapping canvas all around me.

The exercise made me feel hungry and I tried to find the French long-life bread to make a toasted sandwich. It eluded me. I could remember putting it on board, but where? The crust of the other bread had gone mouldy but it appeared all right inside so I just ate the middle; I don't suppose a bit of mould did much harm anyway.

Later I ran the engine to charge the batteries. I sat by the oil pressure gauge because there seemed to be quite a lot of oil in the bilges and I suspected a leak, although the dipstick still showed maximum. It worried me that on removing the oil filler cap I could only see an empty cavity. Was it supposed to be like that? The engine was running very well and the gauge was steady, so I gave up after a while and reflected that my lack of engine knowledge could prove embarrassing if anything actually went wrong.

5
EARLY SETBACKS IN BISCAY

The next day I wrote in my log: 'Last night and today have really been awful.' I couldn't write earlier because I was unable to put on paper what I felt at the time. It was blowing a gale and one thing after another happened, making me feel that disaster had struck. The first thing was at 2 a.m. when I felt the boat head up into the wind and lurch over. It was blowing about forty knots, typical Bay of Biscay stuff, and I had earlier reduced to a small staysail. I jumped up on deck, pulled the wheel around and heard a 'graunch' which to my horror seemed to be coming from the main rudder. I swung the wheel a few times to see if *Crusader* would respond. She did, and the noise seemed also to have stopped. Just as I was beginning to feel some cautious relief, I heard a banging noise down under the boat. Well, this is it, I said aloud, too stupefied to realize that the noise was actually coming from behind me. When I finally looked behind at the self-steering gear I saw the rudder of the Sailomat was hanging by its safety rope and banging against the servo oar.

By lying flat on my stomach I was just able to pull the rudder inboard, but when I tried to take off the cylinder link from the gearbox, I found the pin connecting it had twisted and seized solid. I tried again with a hammer and a pair of pliers and – of all the stupid things – I freed the pin but *dropped* the vital link the rudder had been attached to. I couldn't believe my eyes as I watched it sinking slowly out of sight. I still had the hammer in one hand; the pliers and the remaining half of the broken pin in the other, but I had let go the thing that most mattered; my feelings of self-reproach were excruciating.

Still, it was no good crying over spilt milk, I told myself, and got on with the job of lowering sail and securing everything on deck in anticipation of bad weather. But one mistake invariably follows another, and the next was to cost me an afternoon's dangerous work. In an attempt at securing the foresail on deck I reached up to unclip the halyard. It was then I soon realized that I couldn't reach it without standing up, while to stand up meant risking being thrown off the pitching foredeck. It would be safer, I decided, to leave the halyard clipped on and tie the sail down as best I could. This I did, and I tightened up the halyard on the mast winch to prevent it from flaying. The next morning when I came on deck I saw how foolish this was, for in the night the halyard had unclipped itself from the sail and was now wrapped round the spreaders, the shrouds, the flag halyard and the aerial. I would have to climb the mast to retrieve it.

The halyard was about a third of the way up the mast – I could see the end of it just below the spreaders. I waited until mid-day when I fancied the wind had eased, put on my oilskins and safety harness and started up the mast, clipping and un-clipping myself at each step. The lurching of the boat was far more pronounced aloft, and it seemed to be making a deter-mined attempt to throw me off. I finally reached the end of the halyard and freed it from the spreaders. I gave it a tug hoping to pull it down, but it remained stuck. A nice kettle of fish. I couldn't see what to do from my present position, and anyway my head was spinning, so I climbed back down to the deck to think the problem out. But thinking doesn't come easily when a boat is dancing wildly and one is feeling seasick. Finally, I managed to work out a plan: climb as far as the spreaders, grab hold of the end of the halyard, fling it over the spreaders, catch it, pass it around the cap shrouds, untwirl it four times around the forestay and then . . . but, wait a minute – there was a flaw in this crazy operation. At some point in the performance I should have to let go, and then what? It would twist itself around something *else*! Still, I should have to try. So up the mast I went once again, not clipping myself on to each step this time but rather trusting to luck and a good hold and, in consequence, getting up considerably faster. Once aloft I tied myself to the mast with my harness lifeline and attempted to throw the halyard end over the spreaders, carefully timing the throw with the period of the boat's roll so that I would be able to catch it as it returned. But it was no use; I still couldn't free the halyard. However, I was learning – before my descent I tied a spare line to the end of the errant halyard so that I shouldn't have to climb so high the next time; meanwhile, I went below to lie on my bunk and recover my equilibrium. Late in the afternoon I did bring the halyard end down from the mast and in a grip that nearly throttled it.

All this time *Crusader* had been sailing along nicely by herself, but in the wrong direction. Another arduous job was demanded – that of attaching the spare rudder to the Sailomat. By the end of the afternoon I was moving again in the right direction but feeling thoroughly dejected – only six days out, I said to myself, and this is the trouble I run into.

That evening I called Rob's father and asked him to pass a message to Sailomat requesting them to send a spare rudder to the Canary Islands for me. This was my rendezvous as arranged with the *Daily Express*, and I hoped to be there in a week's time. The news that Rob was maintaining good speed cheered me, and by the time I had cooked a tea of boiled potatoes, boiled beetroot and poached eggs I had regained my spirits completely.

Thursday, and one week out from Dartmouth, was a most productive day. I spent several hours sealing the aft hatch cover where I suspected the water in the bilges had entered. I'd been counting the strokes of the bilge pump every day so I'd soon know if this was the culprit. I knew that all boats leaked from one source or another, and that you must expect to have to pump the bilges a little every day. Just the same, I thought *Crusader* was taking in more water than was normal. Also I tightened the stern gland (where the propeller shaft passes through the hull) as it seemed to be dripping too much.

After I'd done that I suddenly remembered where I'd put the long-life bread. I'd turned the boat inside out looking for it, and there it was underneath the bin where all the sacks of fruit and vegetables were stored, the heaviest things in the boat. Whatever possessed me to put it there? I took yet another piece of skin off my hands re-stowing the vegetables, and later in the day permitted myself the luxury of using fresh water to wash them. My hands were getting into a sorry state with several cuts which didn't seem to be healing very well – probably because they were in salt water so often. They were also well ingrained with dirt; washing hands in salt water is not very successful – especially when it is cold. This time I tried a good, hot, soapy wash and then had a manicure. It made a great difference, and I thought my hands looked quite respectable again.

The wind had now gone light, following the rough weather of the day before, and so I changed to bigger sails. But no sooner had I got them hoisted than the wind sprung up and I had to dash forward to drop them again. Damn! The wind speed had gone from nothing to twenty-five knots in a matter of seconds. Laboriously I lowered the mainsail, reefed it, changed to a smaller yankee . . . and then the wind disappeared again. Very annoying. For the rest of the day the wind went up and down like a yo-yo; sometimes boisterous at twenty-five knots; other times just a zephyr. With a full crew it would have been possible to keep up with the changes – and necessary, too, when racing – but I was alone with 30,000 miles to go, and working like a maniac putting sails up and down to suit every wind strength would have been a lot of hard work for not much gain. But nevertheless I should have made the effort since progress generally had been slow; I'd sailed about 700 miles but could only count 600 miles of them in the right direction.

I found myself thinking about the incident of the halyard and the trouble that can arise through carelessness (or bad seamanship). I was glad – now that it was over – that I had been up the mast and had nothing worse than bruises to show for it. In harbour the prospect of such action had frightened me, and I never imagined that I should ever really have to climb aloft. It was Chay who suggested having steps riveted on to the mast just in case, and how pleased I was that we did so. How Robin Knox-Johnson and Sir Francis Chichester managed without steps I can't imagine, although I remember that Chichester never did go up the mast – the result of his good seamanship and good fortune, I suppose.

As for the safety harness it just wasn't practical to clip it on all the time. It slowed me down enormously, not only when climbing the mast but on deck as well. Rob had told me that in the first Whitbread Round the World Race he had used a harness very infrequently because it was an encumbrance when quick action was demanded. My situation was different; I wasn't racing, and critical situations wouldn't happen so often I hoped. But I was still very conscious of the danger of falling overboard. I felt vulnerable much of the time on deck although I didn't believe a harness was the answer. Better to be careful, constantly watchful and continually aware of the danger.

15 September (Day 7)
I've just had a horrible fright. I was looking at the self-steering gear trying to work out where the slight, but now continual, creaking noise was coming from when I saw a crack in the main holding bracket! It's a wonder that it hasn't come right apart. I've roped it to the rails which may not keep it together but will save it from falling into the sea if it does not break away completely.

I was due to make a call to the *Daily Express* that afternoon so I included a second urgent message to Sailomat, this time requesting a spare bracket.

I continually marvelled at how easy it was to talk to people in England; they often sounded as clear as if I were calling them across the street. I limited my calls to one every three days; after the Canaries I should have to content myself with one a week as the radio used so much battery power. Calling home wasn't so important to me since Rob wasn't there, although it was the only way I could get news of him. Still, there was abso-lutely nothing I could do if he should be in any trouble. Three people had died in the first Round the World Race; racing big yachts in heavy seas for months on end is a sport which involves large risks. I dared not think of anything happening to Rob; I depended on him to be *somewhere* – it wasn't even important that I knew where exactly, as long as he was waiting for me so that one day, in the dim future, we could continue our life together.

The *Daily Express* was anxious to know how the photography was going, so I assured them I'd taken hundreds of beautiful shots. As soon as I was off the radio I got out the camera to figure out how it worked. The purpose of the rendezvous at the Canary Islands was for me to hand over the films, the movie film for ITN and a written piece on my progress. In turn I would receive mail and, hopefully, the spares that Sailomat were flying out. I wouldn't be calling into port – the idea was for the rendezvous boat to meet me at sea.

The weather was warmer now – I was off the coast of Portugal but keeping well out to sea as the tides are strong near a coast. It was good to be able to wear shorts and T-shirts on deck and no longer experience the cold shock when spray splashed over me.

Boris was venturing on deck and exploring his upstairs territory. He was steady on his feet but, I thought, much too inquisitive for his own good. When the boat was becalmed the sheets would flop up and down as the sail filled with wind and then collapsed, and Boris was determined to find out what caused this strange phenomenon. He was so taken with it that, every time I took him below to try and distract him, he would ignore whatever it was I was trying to interest him in and return to examining the sheets. I would hold my breath as he balanced on the toe rail around the boat's edge and reached up to hit the sheet with his paw. How can I warn him? I wondered. I did think of lowering him over the edge into the water just to let him know there was something nasty down there, but if he'd struggled and got free I'd never have forgiven myself. I had to let him have the run of the deck in calm weather so that he would get used to it; it would only have made his life a misery if I had harnessed him to anything. I simply hoped the novelty of the moving sheets would eventually diminish. Meanwhile the precarious situations he contrived worried me, and I got into the morbid habit of coming on deck and first of all looking for him in the wake.

I wished the days were longer. The light never seemed to last very long, and I was reluctant to use the batteries. There were still many jobs to be done, and I invariably worked all day – occasionally taking time off to set up a camera and take shots of what I was doing. Water was still getting into the bilges, so I sealed off the cockpit lockers hoping to make them stormproof in the bad weather that would eventually arrive. I wasn't yet thinking as far ahead as the Roaring Forties, but there was the possibility of a gale or two in the 6000 miles or so I still had to go before reaching the higher latitudes. Another important job was to secure all the heavy objects on board, like the flexible fuel tank and the life raft. This meant drilling holes, fitting eye-bolts and making shock-cord webbing to hold them.

The sun was too hot for me to be on deck for long periods, nevertheless I did spend four hours one day replacing the entire basic unit of the self-steering gear with the spare one. I was pleased with the result; it seemed to function better, and the exercise made me more familiar with the workings of this extraordinary but faithful piece of equipment. There weren't many repair jobs left to do on deck by now but still a few down below. Andrew had cautioned me to grease the steering occasionally, so I climbed into the aft hatch with the grease pot and stared at the array of steel arms and legs that made up the boat's main steering system. After looking at it for a while I still wasn't sure what needed attention, so I simply put some grease on the parts that looked already greasy: a messy job considering I didn't have a grease gun and had to use my fingers. Yuk!

Andrew had also told me to look after the batteries. I had three beautiful, brand-new batteries, and I was determined they wouldn't suffer the same fate as those that I'd seen when Chay took over the boat. I was going to treat my batteries with loving care. Boris decided to help me and got 'anti-corrosive' grease all over his feet which he didn't care for greatly.

The days passed quickly and uneventfully. There was remarkably little wind, and I had to dig out my lightest and largest sail, the ghoster, and set it on the forestay. Even with that sail I was still only averaging one and a half to two knots! There was about 1000 square feet of sail in the ghoster but, of course, it was very light cloth and no effort to hoist. The genoa, which was my next biggest foresail, was really quite a handful and big enough I suppose to cover the roof of the average family house. Getting it down in a strong wind was the devil's own job. I never seemed to have enough arms and legs and would invariably end up fighting my way out of its voluminous folds as it collapsed around me on the foredeck. If too much of it fell in the sea, that was worse; then it might take as much as ten minutes to recover, while the ocean and I tugged for possession. And by then I'd have aching arms and be completely out of puff. But there wasn't much of an alternative. I had chosen a 53-foot boa which had to have large sails to push it along, and I could hardly complain about the effort needed to handle them. At least, unlike the racing crews, I had plenty of time to make sail changes, and I didn't have to leave a sail set until the maximum wind was reached (when it was likely to blow out). I always stayed inside that limit, changing to smaller sails earlier; consequently I never suffered any serious sail damage.

In the light and variable winds of those days the off-course alarm buzzed long and persistently – till one day it fell silent. I opened up the instrument housing and gave it a few pokes which prompted it to work a little longer, but it shortly gave up altogether. Much as I disliked it, I didn't expect it to show me this lack of consideration; I now had to waken myself up every hour or so to check the course. However, I soon became conditioned to this new situation and found that even when I didn't set the alarm, I woke about every hour and a half. To make it easier to check the course I set up my spare compass on the saloon table and then only had to sit up in my bunk and shine the torch on it.

On Day 12 I saw a number of ships which confirmed that I was on a parallel with Lisbon. I was moving swiftly at last. The previous day's run had brought me to within 350 miles of the Canaries, and I started to think about approaching land; it seemed now as if I might actually get there! I contacted the *Daily Express* and gave them my ETA (Estimated Time of Arrival). They were anxious for me to be there in the daytime so that they could take photographs.

I spent most of my time during these hot days down below reading and writing letters. My favourite place to sit was by the chart table; here I could prop myself against a cushion on the bulkhead and put my feet on the table.

For a few days, at certain moments, I had been startled by an odd noise which sounded like a bee trapped in a jar. It was as if the ghost of the off-course alarm was moving down the electrical wires from the instrument box and disappearing into the back of the chart table. I listened closely to the wires until logic decreed that the sound couldn't possibly be coming from the wires, although I couldn't think of any other explanation. Thoughts of the Bermudan Triangle passed through my mind, but then I reasoned that if any strange beings from outer space (or darkest Russia) were going to manifest themselves, they wouldn't do so as a buzz in a bottle. The noise disappeared one afternoon but next morning it was back again. It seemed to be coming from the drawer beneath the chart table. I opened it and finally ran the ghostly buzzing to ground. It was my little chronometer! I picked it up and stared in disbelief. But there was no mistake – the thing was buzzing. Then I noticed a small 'alarm' button on the side. I must have set it off a few days before by mistake. After the event, I was disappointed that this eerie problem could have such a mundane solution.

21 September (Day 13)

Calms again, how boring. I'm now 280 miles from Lanzarote but not going very fast. I've worked out the sun's amplitude to check my compass and discover the error is 9° high. [Later in the trip I was to learn a great deal about compass error; the 9° error that I had cleverly worked out was correct, but only by a fluke.] I have high hopes of finding Lanzarote!

Two days later I rang the *Daily Express* to learn they were worried about making the rendezvous – I wasn't. I wrote at the time:

If they fail to turn up or if the weather's bad that's just hard luck – I'm going on. I refuse to call into port unless it's absolutely necessary, and while I want those parts for the self-steering gear and my letters, I'll sacrifice them all if needs be.

I took sun-sights in the afternoon which put me about forty miles north-west of the island of Fuerteventura. I altered course slightly to approach the middle of the island and hoped to be about twenty miles off the coast at daylight. I didn't see any lights in the night but then remembered that there were no towns on that side of the island, although the knowledge didn't prevent me from feeling nervous. Early in the morning I peered anxiously into the haze, willing land to appear. As the sun rose the haze slowly lifted and I felt a shock of surprise and pleasure as a craggy coastline slowly took shape underneath.

I wrote exuberantly in my log: 'Land ! ! I've found it!' It was such a pleasure to find that my navigation was all right, I felt like the cat that swallowed the canary. I tried immediately to get a call through to England despite the early hour, but I was drowned out by a million other early risers. I sailed at a good speed along the coast of Fuerteventura but didn't see the island of Gran Canaria, where the rendezvous was to take place, until mid-afternoon. It lay on my starboard bow, and when the heading was right I gybed and set course for Las Palmas. I eventually got through to the *Daily Express* in London but by this time it was too late to make the rendezvous on that day. I probably wouldn't reach the outer harbour of Las Palmas till after dark, and I asked the *Express* to pass this message to the photographer who was waiting on the island.

I sailed slowly up to the top of the island and then took the sails down and lay-a-hull till daylight. I was a bit disgruntled at the waste of time and kept thinking how I could have been past Las Palmas by now and heading for South Africa. But I'd agreed to a daylight meeting so I had to curb my impatience. By early light I was heading towards the lighthouse on the northern tip of the island. I saw now that I had lain off further than necessary and it was nine o'clock before I was within a mile of the light tower. My small-scale chart didn't show which side of a thin peninsula I had to go to reach the harbour, so I called up the coastguards and asked. They told me I should go to the east side. Conveniently I also spoke to the photographer who was waiting at the coastguard station. I told him it would take me two hours to reach the rendezvous point, and we agreed that the boat should accompany me down the coast for a few miles.

Exactly two hours later I weaved my way through the anchored ships clustered around the harbour entrance and looked for the rendezvous boat. There was nothing that remotely looked like one, other than a pilot launch buzzing back and forth between the cargo ships. I could neither go in through the entrance nor stay where I was, so I continued slowly past the harbour wall, each moment expecting to see a small boat filled with smiling faces. But nothing appeared, and I was beginning to feel very annoyed.

Three hours later I was five miles past the entrance, hove-to and was so angry I could have murdered someone. I could still see the harbour entrance and was certain no boat had come out. There was no answer from the coastguard and I wept tears of frustration and rage; I could have been clear of those damned islands by now and heading for the Cape of Good Hope.

The sea was rising, and the wind had turned and was now blowing straight out of the harbour mouth; it would have taken me hours to beat back and besides, by then it would probably have been dark. Imagine waiting all that time for people who had only to come half a mile, while I had journeyed over 1600 miles to meet them! I have never felt so wild in my life or known such helpless frustration.

Finally I radioed the *Daily Express* in London. They had no idea what went wrong and a new rendezvous point was arranged twenty miles further south. It meant another miserable night hove-to in a strong and gusty wind with little opportunity to sleep, but I needed those spares and I did, I realized, have an obligation to the newspaper.

The rendezvous, which at one time I had looked forward to, was not a happy event, and I could hardly bring myself to speak to the photographer. I posed for the photographs, tried to smile, picked up my spares, handed over the films and then was rather surprised and disappointed to see there were no letters for me – I didn't know till months later that my letters had not been brought out to the rendezvous.

6

LOST TO THE OUTSIDE WORLD

Away from the island and into clear water my spirits rose immeasurably. That afternoon I wrote in my log:

> Cape Town, here I come! Gran Canaria is still just visible in the distance, damn it. I wouldn't care if I never laid eyes on it again – unless it's on the way home, of course! The wind is blowing between twenty and thirty knots and I have only the reefed main and staysail set, but the combination seems good. The barometer is falling, I wonder what's to come? I feel better having the spares, but if that's what rendezvous are like, then that will be the first and the last.

Then I saw the lighter side and laughed when I remembered how Boris had reacted to the rendezvous boat. He was interested in all things at a distance, but this time when a boat actually came alongside, his hackles rose and he bolted down below and into an empty locker where he hid, and he refused to come out until the boat had disappeared.

Towards evening the wind became light and variable. In an effort to put as many miles as possible between myself and the land I worked hard changing sail, and by nightfall I was rewarded by no longer having the Canary Islands in sight.

I was not able to sleep very much that night due to shipping activity, and I felt haggard by the morning. But as I stood on deck in the bright early sunshine I was cheered that I had at least been able to *find* the islands. It made me much happier about navigation, and I felt confident now that I would be able to find the Cape of Good Hope. Ahead of me lay over 6000 miles of empty ocean – at least it was deserted along the track I had chosen to follow; that was the curving 'trade route' used by old sailing ships. A rhumb-line to Cape Town would mean passing through a gigantic high pressure zone that meant little wind and very slow sailing.

In the afternoon of Day 20 I wrote in my log:

This really is the most exasperating weather I've ever come across. One minute there is no wind at all and, minutes later, it's blowing between twenty to thirty knots. So far today I've done fourteen sail changes! Oddly enough, there are no clouds to be seen; most peculiar conditions. But the speed is good and I'm going in the right direction, and I might be able to get some more sleep tonight if the wind would just stop going up and down. I had a large feed of fried potatoes, peas, eggs and gherkin at two o'clock which will probably do me until tomorrow. I don't appear to have lost any weight since I started in spite of the exercise and irregular mealtimes.

On Day 21 I complained in my log of too little sleep, tender hands, too many ships and too little wind. I decided I needed a treat and put in a call to Rob's father and Maureen. I learnt that *Great Britain II* was farthest south of all the yachts but hadn't yet picked up the westerly winds they were searching for. Their ETA at Cape Town was about three weeks away, on the 5th or 6th of October (they were going almost twice as fast as I was). Maureen told me that Chay was sailing *Great Britain III*, the trimaran, across the Altantic in an attempt to break the speed record – he had waited for a gale before setting off which seemed strange, yet logical, I suppose. It gave my spirits a great lift to hear all the news.

After the phone call I decided what I wanted just then was a grapefruit. I hadn't eaten any before because they keep longer than other fruit, but now I really fancied one. There was a rather ominous smell coming from the fruit and vegetable bins, so I decided to sort them out and throw away the rotten and the suspect. I cleared the biscuits and the disposable kitchen towels, which had been curiously placed on top of the potatoes, and I finally came to the nub of the smell. And, sure enough, when I lifted up a heavy bag the bottom dropped out along with the most nauseating mess of rotting potatoes.

I disappeared to find my rubber gloves. Armed with these and a dustpan I approached the bin once more. The smell was now so revolting that I retreated retching. But something had to be done or I should have had to abandon ship; I took a deep breath and dived into the evil sticky mess again. It was one of the most horrible jobs I have ever had to tackle. After I'd cleared up, I washed the locker with disinfectant and sorted out the rest of the fruit and vegetables. The other bag of potatoes was fine, so were the grapefruit and oranges and some of the apples.

I was now so dirty that I threw away my clothes as I couldn't spare the fresh water to wash them, then washed myself and put on some talcum powder. I was not quite sure what talcum powder was for, but I supposed that with its rather overpowering smell it must have some use other than caring for babies' bottoms. I was right. It not only made me feel clean, but its fragrance took over from the smell of rotten potatoes. The cabin too was clean once more, and the grapefruit was delicious.

The next day, Day 22, I did the last big job oustanding. I fixed the main hatch door so that I could fasten it properly and be reasonably watertight within. There were still one or two other bad weather precautions to take, such as rearranging the galley benches and stowing various food items. I could imagine what a mess there would be if the milk and other stuff were to be dislodged and land in the radio opposite.

I next inspected my electronic instruments, or rather I took out the little desiccator tubes to see if they had turned pink due to any dampness. The label said that if they *were* pink – and I found they were – to put them in an airing cupboard until they returned to their natural blue. I didn't have an airing cupboard (not many boats do) so I put them in a casserole dish in the oven. Unfortunately, I became tied up with something else after that and when I rushed to get them out they'd all gone funny and black – well and truly cooked, in fact. Luckily, I had a spare desiccator, so from then on I had to shuffle it back and forth between instruments depending on which looked the most damp.

1 October (Day 23)

A new month, that's good. Quite good progress, too – about 147 miles yesterday and 120 today. The wind has died but the sea is still lumpy, which makes *Crusader* roll unpleasantly. At times the genoa and mainsail hang loose or the genoa backs and flaps like a demented goose.

The wind had been strong for a few days and I thought at last I had reached the expected 'trade winds'. But then it swung round to the NW and died, rose again and died, and so on until I wondered if I was in the wrong part of the ocean. Mindlessly I thought about abandoning ship, and I thought I'd check on my survival kit, which was positioned by the hatchway door. It took me the whole morning to reorganize the kit, and it gave me an eerie and unpleasant sensation, especially when I came to remind myself to take along the boat-hook to ward off sharks – I wondered if it wouldn't annoy them instead. Some of my 'abandon ship' stores were in a large bin by the hatch steps. Here I had such things as tinned peaches, fruit juice, steak pies, cream, goulash, a heavy plastic bag with my medical kit, fog horn, lengths of rope, salt-water evaporator, heliograph, ten large bars of chocolate, medical hand cream and a few other bits and pieces. Also several bags of clothes, sealed against the damp. A life-jacket and a harness were on top. Under the steps and ready to grab were the distress flares, short-range emergency radio and a five-gallon can of water. It amounted to quite a pile of equipment to be taken off in a hurry. I decided the order of priorities, made a list and pasted it above the hatch door. When faced with the decision to leave the boat, one wouldn't want to start thinking about what to take off first.

Sometime after leaving the Canaries I began to lose track of time. Although I wrote the date each day in my ship's log, I wasn't aware of days in the usual sense; there was nothing to distinguish Thursday from Sunday, for example, and so it was some surprise on 4 October to discover that a week had gone by since the rendezvous. I could expect no human contact (except via the radio) for the next two and a half months when there would probably be another rendezvous off Cape Town.

To most people the daunting feature of this voyage would have been the length of time spent alone. To me that wasn't important at all as I can very well do without people. This must have something to do with my nature, but it is not altogether unconnected with the years I spent in close contact with the trivial and superficial aspects of human nature – especially in hairdressing. One evening I must have been thinking particularly vehemently on the subject for I wrote in my log:

> I've heard people say that so-and-so doesn't suffer fools gladly. Well, eventually I learnt to suffer fools because I didn't want to lay myself open to criticism. But all that niceness I had to generate drove me to further extremes of dislike. Now I find that I don't even have the patience to talk over the trivialities of life with people I find as uninteresting as their topics of conversation. This more than anything has driven me to prefer silence because I don't have the strength of mind or the lack of manners to tell people I'm bored to death by their pettiness. This must sound arrogant, but I see no possibility of any worthwhile relationship developing with certain sorts of people.
>
> It is interesting to speculate how the voyage will affect me. I don't think that it is likely to make me more gregarious, though this doesn't mean I dislike *all* people; on the contrary, there are people who interest me enormously. and in whose company I find great pleasure, albeit in small doses. And of course there is Rob, with whom I could spend every minute of my life in perfect ease. Perhaps for this reason I don't find being apart from him such a terrible tribulation – as long as it is of my own choosing. He is now a part of me and I don't need his presence as a constant reminder. With him I am happy – together or apart.
>
> Rob, on the other hand, *is* gregarious; he likes people and makes friends easily. He has a warm and outgoing personality, which is very fortunate for me because he has provided me with a back to hide behind when the social going gets rough.

Now that I'd got over the trauma of leaving and had settled into the routine of living aboard my 53-foot home, I found myself thinking more about the past,

My mind drifted back over the years I'd spent in Europe, especially those years in Vienna which had purged me of most of my soul-searching. That was fortunate for now, with so much time to think, I might otherwise have plunged into an orgy of despair over the state of the universe or the future of mankind or some such thing. Now, as I sat at the chart table and sipped a sweet martini, I was glad those years of turmoil were behind me. My world had become very small and – if one could ignore the elements – quiet and peaceful. The world could blow up and I wouldn't be any the wiser or even particularly worried. Again the question arose, is this escapism? I didn't care; the world and its inhabitants were too remote for their opinions to be considered, and since I hadn't yet reached the stage of answering myself back during these deliberations, I also wasn't likely to be contradicted.

These reflections were invariably interrupted by a change in the wind, or by my stomach reminding me that there were more important things to think about than philosophy. Besides, I didn't spend all my quiet moments thinking. I had several hundred books, mostly novels or autobiographies and a dozen or so about art and antiques. After nearly a month at sea and with the longest and worst part of the journey still ahead, I wanted to read autobiographies of the adventurous kind: books such as, *Annapurna, South Face*, by Chris Bonington, and *Seven Years in Tibet*, by an Austrian prisoner of war. These and the single-handers' books were in a way parallels, and I was searching for likenesses and comparisons. I was surprised to read that Chris Bonington's reasons for his attempt on Annapurna were almost exactly the same as my motives for wishing to sail around the world:

The satisfaction of exploring new ground . . . and perhaps even more important, of exploring one's own reactions to new, at times exacting, experience. There is the sheer beauty and grandeur of the mountains, the soothing balm of solitude. And through it all, is the undercurrent of danger: for this is what climbing is all about; staking one's life on one's judgement, playing the calculated risk. This doesn't mean going blindly into danger, or seeking hazard for its own sake. The climber gains his satisfaction from going into a potentially dangerous situation but then, through his own skill and experience, rendering it safe.

To me, his adventure sounds more hazardous and frightening than mine, but then perhaps he might not agree. Each to his own; perhaps a ton of threatening, crashing water on a rolling foredeck would horrify him as much as looking down a vertical wall of ice would mortify me. It was, of course, the survival element which was common to both ventures, and it was this which gave even the more routine things like sail handling a different flavour – something very different from the sort of danger encountered while crossing a street in central London.

I passed the Cape Verde Islands on 4 October, Day 26, about a hundred miles to the east. But even if I'd passed within ten miles it was doubtful that I would have seen them. They would have been hidden in the fine Sirocco dust that was blowing from the Spanish Sahara. It was everywhere, leaving its coat of orange mess on the deck and on my nice new sails. The weather was incredibly hot – I was almost steaming! Sail changes took twice as long as usual and I panted from the heat, the slightest exertion made my heart beat uncomfortably and I was forced to take long rests, sometimes leaving the sails to drag behind in the water while I rested on the deck, working up the energy to pull them in. I was eating too much, that was obvious, so as a punishment I went without dinner occasionally and didn't have breakfast till late morning. My baker friend, Philip, had provisioned me so well with chocolates, sweets and crisps that I was tempted to eat far more than I usually did. I put in my log:

I mustn't put on weight or Rob will have a fit. But then I'm bound to eat less when the bad weather comes so I'm not really worried. I've just gybed so I must have worked off those five jelly babies I ate earlier. My face is covered in a film of orange dust which makes me look as though I've got an extra dark tan; I feel too lazy to wash it off. Boris is

languishing in the bows, but every now and then he makes a
desperate leap in the air to try and catch the foot of the genoa
as it flaps inboard; his feet hit the top of the guard rails and
he falls back panting to the deck. He got into a box of tissues
last night, tore up half a dozen and scattered the remainder
over the floor. I had previously thrown him off my bunk for
chewing my feet so I suppose he did that to punish me.

Boris didn't enjoy the heat any more than I did but he always
accompanied me on deck for a sail change. I discouraged him
from lying in the sails on deck because I was afraid the wind
might catch them and balloon him over the side. His favourite
trick was to climb up the mast a little way and sit on a winch to
watch me. Either that or dangle upside down in the ropes –
practising for the Antipodes, I suppose he thought. He took to
guarding his territory very seriously, and whenever birds or
flying fish landed on deck they would be speedily and noisily
evicted; often Boris ended up with scales lodged in his teeth or
stuck to his paws.

Most of the time I spent below; it was hotter than up on deck
but away from the sun's glare. If there was a semblance of a
breeze I would leave all the hatches open and ventilate the boat.
The fruit, especially the grapefruit, were marvellous in this
weather as they helped me quench my thirst without the aid of
gallons of water – a commodity I could ill afford to waste. I'd
estimated I'd have enough water to last me the voyage if I used
it merely for drinking tea and cordial (I don't much like coffee).
Then again I could always replenish my supply in the Doldrums
where I knew there were plenty of rain squalls.

—

On the evening of 5 October I put a call through to Rob's father
to find out if Rob had reached Cape Town and if there was a number I could call. I had to stand by the radio for ages before my
turn came but eventually I heard that Rob was due to arrive
the next day. I was thrilled to think that I would soon be talking
to him.

The tail end of the radio call was interrupted by a familiar noise through the hull which meant that dolphins were paying me a visit. Their noisy squeaking was unmistakable. I went on deck to have a look. There was no moon, but the night was clear and the sea was alive with phosphorescence that glittered and gave each creature a fiery tail stream; the dolphins were treating me to some wizardry. They must have a code because with one accord thirty or forty of them would suddenly leap in the air, snort and return with a mighty splash that sent spray over the deck. I laughed and yelled encouragement, as they looked so fantastic. Boris didn't approve; his fur stood on end, and resembling a cactus he fled below. He reappeared later looking suspiciously around the hatch and listening to the squeaks and snorts but obviously he didn't enjoy it much. That afternoon I saw five small whales pass within twenty yards of the stern, but they didn't stop – fortunately Boris didn't see them.

6 October (Day 28)
I had to do a maintenance job on the Sailomat yesterday and although I wore a headscarf I am now suffering from sunstroke. This morning when I got up I could hardly stand – I felt so dizzy. I lay down and wondered if it might be hunger. I felt better after six scrambled eggs and a pickled gherkin but still not completely recovered. I haven't been on deck in the sun today except to gybe, fit a new boom-vang and throw a few buckets of sea water over myself. I also washed my hair and it felt marvellous for a while but soon went sticky again. Other than that I have spent the whole day reading.

The next morning, as arranged, I tried to radio Rob's father. There was a lot of traffic waiting to get through to Portishead, and it was two hours before they could accept my call.

Rob's father told me he had spoken to his son only five minutes earlier. Rob had been beaten to Cape Town by two other yachts and, though disappointed, was glad to be in port again. He had left a number for me to call and said he would be standing by the phone for the next two nights.

I made notes of the things I wanted to talk to Rob about and

generally fiddled around in the afternoon willing the time away.
In case I should have to wait as long again for my Portishead
call to come through I put up the aerial and turned on the set
some two hours before Rob was expecting me. I was all ready to
go, but when I picked up the handset to make the call, nothing
happened. I stared at the radio for a minute, thinking there must
have been something I'd forgotten to do, but no, everything
seemed to be in order and still the radio remained dead.

An hour later I had a sick and desperate feeling. I'd done
everything I could and had no idea what to do next. I couldn't
believe it was a major fault – it just couldn't be, I kept telling
myself. I'd found all the radio spares and changed some fuses,
but to no avail. I washed the deck terminal with fresh water and
even got out the instruction manual – I might as well have tried
to learn Greek in one sitting. I even looked inside the radio, but
that was so alarming I shut it again quickly.

The thought of Rob waiting for my call that night, and perhaps for the next four weeks, made me feel quite desperate. I
racked my brains to see if there was something I'd overlooked,
but there was nothing. I sat in utter dejection till I knew Rob
would have given up waiting for my call. He would presume
I'd not been able to get through and would wait again tomorrow. . . .

Slowly it dawned on me that I still had thousands of miles to
go to Cape Town and unless I could hail a passing ship no one
would know if I were alive or dead. For my own part I never
expected help to come from the radio, but I hated more than
anything else not being able to relieve the anxiety of my family,
who would now be faced with total silence.

7
TRAGIC DAYS IN THE SOUTH ATLANTIC

The effect of the broken radio – the severance of my link with the outside world – didn't fully register until four days after it happened. Up until that time I still believed I could trace the fault and repair it. After all, it was a brand-new radio; it hadn't felt a drop of water, nor spilt tea which the technician had said would be even worse than salt water. I changed every fuse several times and stared hypnotically at the acres of tiny valves and transistors till my mind boggled and I finally had to admit defeat. The second night was worse; I tried not to think of Rob hovering by the phone and becoming more anxious with each hour that passed. I lost my appetite both for food and sleep and spent more time on deck changing sails, thinking that the sooner I got within VHF range of Cape Town the better. I was about 360 miles from Liberia and 700 from the nearest corner of Brazil. I wondered idly about calling into one or other of these places, but that would have meant an enormous diversion, and if I intended to get around Cape Horn I couldn't afford the time. I still had about 5000 miles to go before Cape Town; I wasn't yet halfway.

The broken radio and the anxiety it was causing me, the feckless winds, the miserably slow progress, all these things had contributed to a mood of depression which I seemed unable to throw off. I had read that people frequently suffered such moods in the Doldrums, and it was certainly affecting me. It also began to affect my efficiency; already I had made several careless mistakes, and now I was having to force myself to eat properly.

I had to make a conscious effort to snap out of this state of mind for safety's sake.

The weather came to my rescue – it suddenly turned rough! How it lifted my spirits to see *Crusader* come alive and gobble up the miles again. It was beautiful to see her surging through the waves and occasionally crashing down and sending mountains of spray to glitter in the sunshine. It was impossible to feel downhearted at such a sight, and I was hardly aware of the discomfort or the constant need to hang on and brace myself against the wild and surging movement.

It was in these trade wind conditions that *Crusader* really showed me what she could do. As long as I gave her sufficient canvas she ploughed through the waves effortlessly, occasionally landing hard on a big one and sending tons of water cascading, before she immediately picked up speed again and drove forward. She didn't continually pound as many boats do, and by under-canvassing I could stop her heeling excessively. Chichester, I had read, carried a lot of sail in times like these because *Gipsy Moth* went well when pressed. *Crusader*, I believe, sailed better when upright – or maybe I convinced myself of that because I hated being heeled over. The strains on the mast were much greater when she heeled and, although the mast looked very strong, I was terrified of breaking it. The trouble was that I didn't know if I was pressing her too hard or being too cautious. It added more than a knot if I set the staysail in this sort of wind, but at the same time I could imagine a chain plate ripping out of the deck or the forestay snapping. Maybe my imagination was getting the better of me, but I still had 28,000 miles to go and the equipment had to stay intact.

But in time I grew more used to hard windward sailing and gained more confidence in the rig.

15 October (Day 37)
19.30: I'm thrilled by the way she's sailing at the moment. The sail area is just right for the strength of wind so long as it doesn't fall under twenty-two knots. *Crusader* is no racing machine, but so long as there is sufficient wind she'll average six knots on any point of sailing; perhaps between Cape Town

and Cape Horn I can force the average mileage up.

Later the same day I added:

There is a problem which keeps floating into my consciousness and that is, will they try and persuade me to stop in Cape Town and have the radio repaired? I tried to think what Chay would say. 'Hard luck. You had all the equipment to start with, and if it has broken down that's just too bad – as long as it doesn't impede progress. And, anyway, to hell with the other people, it's your outfit.' Maybe that's not what Chay would say, although it's what I hoped he might say. But what about the *others*? What about Rob, the most important of all; would he have been happy for me to go on without the radio being fixed? I think the answer would be yes. As for my family, I shall just have to have faith in their patience and hope they won't believe the worst.

Thoughts such as these recurred, but I kept them in the back of my mind and concentrated on keeping *Crusader* sailing. The wind was a lot steadier now.

The days are best described as I wrote them at the time:

I am getting more used to strong winds, but it still produces rather odd dreams at night. I have always been prone to vivid dreams, walking and talking in my sleep. Before I set off I often wondered how they would affect me on this trip. I suppose the night I sleepwalk and hoist the ghoster in a force eight will be the time to start worrying!

After jumping out of bed each morning I am now in the habit of checking round the boat. This morning my routine check disclosed a jib sheet pressing against a staunchion, which, in time, would have caused it to chafe through; the jib was sheeted too tightly which meant it wasn't setting very well; another three stiff flying fish in the scuppers and, most disconcerting of all, something wrong with the self-steering gear. There was a pin holding the vane mast to the gear box and, so far as I could see, it had nearly fallen out. I undid the screw and compared it with the spare, but it was undamaged so it must have vibrated loose. I was able to re-tighten it, but now I have another item to watch out for.

My noon-day position tells me that although I have logged 160 miles I have only made 130 miles over the ground. It must be a current setting me back. I'm on the same parallel as the mouth of the Amazon and the island of São Thomé. In fact, I am just about midway between both of them.

It's an interesting thought that if I had suddenly had to make port, I wouldn't have been sure which to head for; choosing between languages wouldn't be difficult as they speak Portuguese in both; I think I'd pick the one with the friendliest crocodiles.

While on deck I watched a small bird with a white bottom flitting among the waves and I wondered what it was. When reading the books, I remember being struck with awe at the vast knowledge of sea birds which most single-handers seem to possess. Many could speak authoritatively of lesser black-backed whatsists, and someone or other's stormy petrels and birds which look like sheep, all of which I hoped to come across. I had fully intended to arm myself with copious volumes of bird books, but in the last-minute rush all I could find in Dartmouth was a book called *The Sea and Oceans* which, though very interesting, didn't contain a reference to a single dicky bird.

On the 16th I crossed the equator, going like a rocket. I'd been especially looking forward to this day because Juliet had put aboard five curious-looking parcels, each marked with the days on which they should be opened. I opened 'Happy First Equator Crossing!' and found a book of short stories by D. H. Lawrence and a sticky lollipop which I immediately ate. Juliet had provided another fifteen or so books to add to my library of 200, but I still wasn't sure if that would be enough. My mother-in-law had given me a fantastic book called *Royal Heritage* which is fat and full of gorgeous picture I could dwell upon and so make the book last, whereas most of the books I consumed in a sitting.

I had a *Concise Encyclopaedia of Antiques*, which was fascinating and also time-consuming. Antiques are a passion of mine, and I spent hours day-dreaming of the house I would like to have, and where the Queen Anne furniture would go . . . and the Rembrandts! In addition to this I had brought pieces of wood from which to carve chess pieces, though I planned to leave this pastime till the weather got cold. I also had several books on navigation and astronomy to amuse me.

In honour of my equator crossing at 17.00 I cooked myself a three-course dinner: vegetable soup, beef with boiled potatoes, onions and peas, and pickled red cabbage, and pineapple slices for 'afters'. This was helped down with a small bottle of best French champagne, and my gloom of the previous day disappeared, along with the empty bottle, to the bottom of the ocean!

Boris also had a share of my dinner and scattered the bits over the chart-room floor as was his usual practice. He looked the picture of a contented cat secure in his own neighbourhood and didn't mind the occasional wild lurch or bang which was so much a part of this strange environment. However, I did shatter his complacency for a moment that afternoon when I dropped the grill pan on the floor close to him. He gazed at me in horror with his fur on end and his mouth full of tuna; I broke the spell by laughing and his hair slowly subsided.

17 October (Day 39)
It is still very hot and as I cannot open the hatches because of the spray it is like a Turkish bath in the cabin. I have then a choice either to steam quietly down below, or come up on deck and get drenched. My favourite position is on the 'bridge', that is to say standing outside the cabin hatchway with my feet on the cockpit seats. From here I can keep a lookout, hold on against the movement and be reasonably sheltered from the spray.

I brought Boris up to the 'bridge' and held him aloft so he could see the reef I had just put in the mainsail. He reviewed my work, but the wind flattened his ears and that was something he didn't appreciate! I find reefing very much easier now, in fact I feel far more confident about handling sails generally and hope that when bad weather comes I shall be able to avoid the catastrophes that arise from inexperience or bad seamanship. However, if anything does go wrong I feel it will be my fault and not *Crusader*'s; she is a marvellous boat and I feel an overwhelming affection for her.

Boris still attempts to walk across the flexible fuel tank. He tries to maintain some dignity, but it is an impossibility while gyrating. I laugh and he looks at me with disdain, then sniffs and stalks off; he doesn't like to be laughed at. He has grown very fussy about his food of late and has insisted on a change of diet. This morning I weakened and gave him some more tuna which he condescended to eat; one of these days you'll be eating corned dog and beans, I told him severely, but he didn't listen.

As I sit in my comfortable seat by the chart table with Edith Piaf singing my favourite French songs and I sip my favourite drink, sweet martini (without the embellishments), I feel a glow of extreme well-being. What's more I've found an excellent tonic for dejection when the weather gets rough – reading a chapter of David Lewis's book, *Ice Bird*! His frightful struggles and his capsize in Antarctica make my journey feel like a summer cruise. I look around and feel I've a long way to go before life becomes that intolerable.

Reading David Lewis reminded me of my own philosophy which I know is trite but still of help to me. It is that when things get bad, they must get better. Situations never stay constant, and sooner or later one snaps out of a black mood and stands up to meet the next problem. But why am I saying this? I've got the whole world, so what have I got to be despondent about?

I had another drama up the mast a couple of days later. When I went to hoist the mainsail after a squall, it jammed and I discovered the spare main halyard was caught across the sail track. I thought it would be easy to clear so I sprinted up the mast (oddly I didn't mind the height at all by then) and tried to free it, but to no avail. So I came down, placed a screwdriver, hammer, pair of pliers and a strip of rubber in a bag, put on a harness and went aloft again. For a while I thought I'd never get it free. Heaven knows how it managed to get wedged where it was, but eventually I managed to free it without too much damage. I came down holding the halyard so that it wouldn't snarl, and I made it up on a cleat. Getting halyards snarled up the mast seemed to be a habit with me.

The next thing to go wrong was the new bilge pump. I fished out the spares, read the instructions and started to take it apart. This much was easy, but it was not so easy to put it back together. It took ages, and then I found there had been nothing wrong in the first place! At any rate the pump appeared to be working again, although I was sure it would play up again before long. With certain mechanical things I had this instinctive feeling that we were not going to get on very well together. The bilge pump was one of them.

As the trade winds pushed *Crusader* swiftly south I thought more and more about the sort of weather I could expect once I hit the higher latitudes. I wouldn't be in the Roaring Forties proper till I passed the Cape of Good Hope, although according to the Pilot book the Southern Ocean depressions can reach up to latitude $30°$ south and occasionally cause severe gales. My thoughts on the subject are recorded in my log on 24 October, Day 46.

At lunch today I started reading Adlard Coles's *Heavy Weather Sailing*, which is a classic on handling small boats in big seas. In the back of my mind was always the problem of what to do in a bad storm. Which is the safest tactic to adopt? The options were to lie-a-hull, run before it, or run before it streaming warps. To lie-a-hull was the most submissive action – that is when all sail is taken down, the wheel lashed and the crew (me) down in the cabin with the door shut. This then allows the boat to bob about on the waves like a cork but, although the tactic is reasonably safe for some boats, I felt *Crusader* heeled too easily. We had lain-a-hull during the Channel storm on our winter trip to the Canaries; that was the time when the engine broke loose as we were knocked down. I wasn't too happy about the idea of lying-a-hull now for if *Crusader* suffered a real capsize the mast might go.

On that winter trip we had also tried running before the storm. This requires putting up the minimum of sail, or possibly having none at all, and just allowing the wind to

blow the boat along. It is the usual tactic with the big fully
crewed yachts, but of course they can always supply a fresh
man to steer; I am alone and can't contemplate being at the
helm for such long periods (in these conditions the self-steering
gear almost certainly would be unable to cope). And steering
is vitally important, for otherwise the boat can be swung
around beam on to the waves and roll over – it could happen
even with somebody steering. The other danger when running
before it, as happened to us, is that a wave can break over
the stern and fill the cockpit – if not most of the boat.

Streaming warps we had never tried. The idea is that by
trailing long heavy ropes over the stern one slows the boat
down and prevents 'broaching', which means veering off
course and ending up beam on to the sea . . . but whatever am
I doing thinking about all this storm drill with the temperature
in the eighties, with a gentle breeze and a beautifully flat, blue
ocean?

Nevertheless, on 25 October I wrote further in my log:

Reading Adlard Coles's book has made me consider attending
to several jobs, and some I have done already. I have put three
bolts in the cover of the batteries box and examined the cockpit
drains. There are two of these and to see how quickly they
drain, in the event of a wave filling the cockpit, I tested them
with two buckets of water. They drained too slowly I thought,
but then there's nothing much I can do about that. I lifted
one of the teak gratings clear of the drains so that I can
get at them instantly if they block. Next I fitted rubber around
the lids of the cockpit lockers to make them thoroughly
watertight. Last year in the Bay of Biscay when we were
pooped, the water got into the cabin and was over the floorboards in a matter of seconds. At the time we thought it had
come through the main hatch which was a poor fit, but I
believe now that most of the water came through the lockers.

The next consideration was to look around and see how many
items would be thrown from their place if the boat were to roll
right over. Geometrically that was quite a difficult thing to
figure out. For example, there are two petrol tins wedged in a
convenient space on the starboard side of the hatchway. They
can't fall forwards, nor they can fall backwards or sideways,

but they can fall *upwards*! So can the water containers and the
flares. Chay won't be very pleased with the number of hooks
and eyes I'm fitting in his boat.

I'm doing a great deal of reading on the subject of storms
(if I had done it during the preparations in England I should
never have left!) and now have a storm plan based on what I
have read, the experience of gales I have had, and what I think
Crusader will most comfortably do. I think because of her
tendency to roll it would be unwise to lie-a-hull in big seas.
The mast *may* stand up to a capsize, but if it didn't then that
would mean the end of the journey. I shouldn't be able to use
my Sailomat, firstly because it might get damaged and secondly
because it probably wouldn't cope with storm conditions. So
that leaves me running before a storm as the only course. I
should probably be able to steer only for a modest period so
would have to get *Crusader* to steer herself, possibly with the
storm jib set, sheeted flat fore and aft.

The dangers that remain are being pooped and broaching.
Now that I've sealed all the cockpit lockers and made the hatch
doors watertight I think she will stand having the cockpit
filled, but I'll remove the gas bottles from the stern locker to
give her extra buoyancy. If the boat begins to go too fast
and surfs down the waves then I shall have think of
something to slow her down, possibly by putting out ropes.
Anyway, all I can do for the present is wait for a gale and see
what happens.

Obviously thinking so much about bad weather was having
an effect on me and also, it seemed, on the weather! My log
extract for 26 October reads:

I glanced out of the window this morning and caught a glimpse
of what looked like a gigantic wave. I hurriedly looked again
and saw that it was a cloud growing up over the horizon like
a giant mushroom, an ominous purple colour and very dense.
I immediately adopted storm tactics. First, I took down the
double-reefed mainsail, raised the staysail and put extra lashings
around the sails on deck. Then I changed the sheet leads on
the storm jib so that I could run down wind if necessary. I
checked that everything was secured and then went below to
tie down my survival kit, companionway ladder, petrol and

water containers. All loose equipment, such as cassette player, sextants and cameras etc., I stowed in drawers and checked the locks and catches. Next, I turned my attention to the galley where I stowed loose items and washed up the inevitable pile of dishes. I had some breakfast after that – fried potatoes, peas and eggs – and settled down to wait.

Within half an hour the cloud had grown into a perfect arc and covered the sky from horizon to horizon. The barometer has been slowly rising for days, but this might be the edge of a new area of low pressure. I wished I could see an overall picture of the area, but I might as well have wished for the stars.

I considered my tactics once more and waited. I was still waiting at mid-day. The wind had increased but it was sporadic – one minute twenty-five knots the next minute nearer forty. Still it was stable enough, so about 4 p.m. I hoisted the mainsail and continued sailing. My cyclone hadn't materialized this time; I suppose I frightened it away.

I hit a period of calm soon after this and with no wind the heat was as bad as it was on the equator; I had to go and throw buckets of sea water over myself to keep cool. I washed my hair in salt water, too, and spared a little fresh water to rinse it. I thought that having to ration fresh water would have bothered me at sea because I normally wash my hair every four to five days. However, I found that it was fine so long as I brushed it, tied it back and didn't study myself in a mirror too often; it didn't feel dirty or itchy.

My appetite had returned, but how I wished I didn't have to eat, it was such a bother. I wrote, 'The sooner someone invents tablet substitutes the better.'

The calm didn't last long, fortunately; the wind returned with gusto and I had to start the whole process of changing from light to heavy sails again.

28 October (Day 50)

Boris and I got a dowsing this morning. When we went on deck I hadn't bothered to put up my oilskin hood, and 1 took a full dollop of sea down my neck. Boris had been perched on the jib winch and he got it as well. He looked shocked and shook himself, but he didn't remove himself below as I thought he would. He looks so funny when he gallops along the heeling deck with his ears flat and his fur fluffed up, but I'm sure he doesn't mind getting wet. He spends many hours gazing down the cockpit drain watching the bits of flotsam gurgle up and down; every now and again he reaches out a paw and tries to grab a piece only to find that the water rushes up the drain and all he gets is a wet foot for his pains.

I feel very pleased with myself for having done a job which I've been putting off through fear that it would prove too difficult. I tightened the belt between the alternator and the engine, because the battery charge needle was flickering too much. To get at the belt was a problem in itself; it meant dismantling part of the engine casing and removing boards from the bulkhead and floorboards. This exposed the belt but didn't allow me enough room. I had to shift the portable generator, several water containers, various pieces of timber and boxes of biscuits. An hour and a quarter later the job was done. I was greasy, sweaty and tired from the feats of contortion, but was happy to have done something which I would never have attempted if there had been a man around. I'm beginning to find that I like tinkering with engines and finding out how they're held together. I subsequently had to have a second wash – two washes in one day was a bit extreme!

When I tested the engine I was annoyed to see that the needle still flickered.

By this time, I imagined Rob would be setting out on the next leg of the race between Cape Town and Auckland, although I didn't know the exact date. If I could get instructions at my next rendezvous on how to fix the radio I might be able to talk to him. I thought how miserable it would be for him having to leave without any news of me.

My position on Day 50 was 27° south and 23° west and still 2000 miles from Cape Town. I estimated I could cover that distance in three weeks or less if I could keep up my average speed of the past month. I hadn't yet decided how I'd approach Cape Town or where my landfall should be; False Bay was a possibility. From there I could contact the shore radio station with my short-range VHF and perhaps get instructions on how to repair my radio telephone. I was a little apprehensive about rounding the Cape because of its reputation for severe weather. Meanwhile, I was still having trouble with the Tilley lamp and I wrote in my log exasperatedly:

> I can't find the instructions for this damned lamp, and I still haven't worked out whether one can use the mantle a second time. After the last attempt I put it away, but dug it out again this evening and tried to light it. I was obviously doing something wrong because I ended up covered in paraffin and although the lamp belched flames and turned black it still refused to light. I am not going to be beaten by some crummy lamp, so I've put another mantle on and will try it again later. I saw an albatross today.

That night I was threatened by another of those funny squalls which looked like cyclones and spent most of the time sitting in my oilskins and boots waiting for it to pass. The barometer was still rising, so I supposed that must mean high pressure somewhere, making it imperative for me to go south and keep out of its way, because high pressure means calms. That squall on the horizon was the slowest-moving thing I had ever seen! But how better to occupy myself than watching its unpredictable progress.

A little later I wrote in my log: 'This squall is all bark and no bite, I think, so I'm going back to bed.'

The next morning, at eight o'clock, Boris went over the side.

8
FEELINGS OF INSECURITY

After a senseless search of two and a half hours I sat down at the chart table and forced myself to write the following:

> Boris has gone. I feel numb and unable to think straight, but I'm going to write this down so that I can begin to accept that it has happened and there's nothing more I can do. Nothing. Shortly after breakfast, I was on the foredeck getting the ghoster ready to hoist when I saw him doing his daredevil act of walking on the toe rail around the boat's edge. I reached out to pull him back, but he came in voluntarily; then I must have turned away. A few minutes later, out of the corner of my eye, I saw him lurch – as he had done several times before – but this time he went over. I saw him hit the water and I rushed to the stern to disconnect the self-steering gear and put the wheel hard over. Then I dashed to the mast to let go the mainsail and staysail halyards. I could see him in the wake about fifty yards away and *Crusader* was slowly turning around towards him. But then I had to go below to start the engine and although it took only a matter of seconds, when I got back to the wheel he had disappeared. When I was past the place where I'd seen him last, I cut the engine, called and listened. There was nothing to be seen or heard. I called and called like a fool and steered the boat round in circles, but it was no use and eventually I told myself to stop. It was so calm and there were barely more than a few ripples on the surface, but Boris was nowhere to be seen.

For a long while afterwards I sat on the stern and just stared at the water, my mind in a turmoil of remorse and my thoughts transfixed by the sheer horror of what had happened. If only I could have found him, I said again and again; there must have been something more I could have done.

After a time I roused myself to go and finish hanking on the ghoster and slowly, reluctantly, hoisted it. With a sense of unreality I watched that sunflecked, seemingly different piece of ocean drift away and finally disappear over the horizon.

The effects of that morning were immediate and far-reaching.

30 October (Day 52)
I've just finished something which I've been meaning to do since the outset, and losing Boris has at last frightened me into action. I've looped long thin ropes down either side of the boat to act as a life-line. The ends are trailing about twelve feet off the stern, which gives me a fighting chance if I go over. There'll be a certain amount of drag from the ropes that will affect my speed but they are thin, and, anyway, it's a matter of deciding on priorities.

I spent the whole day in feverish activity; anything to take my mind off Boris. There were three large gas bottles in the stern locker which I took out and re-stowed in the forward cabin where the kitty litter had been – I threw away the litter. All the tins of cat food went over the side and in their place I put boxes of Pepsi and beer from the cabin floor. I sorted all the tools and spares and put some of them into new boxes. Then I swept the floor of the chart room with a brush and cleared all the hidden nooks and crannies. The sails also came under attack, and I fiddled with the sheets of the mainsail, genoa and staysail until I thought *Crusader* was sailing faster.

The weather began to change and there seemed to be the threat of a gale which forced me to hoist storm sails later in the afternoon. At one stage the wind indicator shot up to sixty knots, but there wasn't really *that* much wind so I thought it simply must have panicked temporarily. It grew cooler and miserably grey and damp. That evening I lit a candle, sat at the chart table and tried to read.

I was reluctant to go to bed in case I started thinking too much about Boris and couldn't sleep. I watched the water dripping off my oilskins and running in little rivulets over the floor, and I thought how lucky I was to have a boat big enough to keep wet oilskins out of the way. The boat was spacious, as it was designed for a crew of ten, yet even so a year's supply of food for one person filled her to capacity; the provisions filled all the lockers, drawers and top berths in the main saloon. I still had plenty of room in which to walk about, but space in itself was a danger since I could fall that much further in rough weather. Fortunately the few times I was thrown I managed to grab at something as I flew past and that partially broke my fall. I had plenty of solid wooden handles placed at arms' length throughout the boat and any progression was always made carefully from one to the other. I gathered a few nasty bruises during the nine months but luckily never had to make use of my inflatable splints.

The next evening I was sitting at the chart table and glaring at a load of evil little gnats helping themselves to my martini. I had the genoa boomed out (I was getting better at that job now) and *Crusader* was gently rolling along, waggling her stern at the small waves behind her. I'd just finished making a rope ladder which I had attached over the stern and suspended just clear of the water. Losing poor Boris had made me morbidly safety conscious, and I was worried about how to get back on board if I fell over. The sides were much too high to climb – I knew that because we'd tried it in the Canaries when we went swimming. Even with the aid of a ladder it would be difficult to get back on board, but at least I'd done all I could to give myself a fair chance of survival. However, it was much more important to make sure I didn't go over in the first place. I always walked around the deck in a sort of crouch, rather like an ape, ready to grab hold of something firm or drop to the deck if the boat gave a lurch. I stepped carefully over or around the sheets, especially the lazy sheets, and treated them as if they were poisonous snakes that might leap up and bite me. I don't think I ever went up on deck without saying to myself, 'Take care and watch what you're doing'.

It would have been easy to have succumbed to the feelings of loss and distress I felt at losing Boris, but I knew I couldn't afford to do that. So I forced myself not to think about him while it was still so painful. Fortunately, I was not totally demoralized by his absence – probably because I wasn't essentially a 'cat lover' and didn't depend on him to overcome loneliness. On the whole I had only noticed he was around when he made his presence felt, although I must say he did that pretty often. He was a dear little cat and he spent his short life on board very happily. Sadly his nature proved too inquisitive and too bold for his environment.

My 55th night at sea was memorable. I had the mainsail and genoa 'goose winged' in the following wind and had to keep getting up every hour to check that they were coping. I sensed the wind was increasing and, sure enough, by 2 a.m. it was proving too much for the light-weather genoa. Somehow or other I had to get it down, and as it was boomed-out that was no easy matter. The boat was rolling heavily which made it precarious although fortunately I could see what I was doing because the moon was up. I altered course to 'spill' some wind from the sail and let go the genoa halyard. The sail stuck aloft because I hadn't eased the sheet sufficiently and I had to go back to the cockpit to do it. Most of the sail then landed in the sea; however, despite the tussle and the deafening noise of flapping sail cloth I was eventually able to get the sail into its bag. Now there was the pole to worry about. This was fixed to the mast on a heel arrangement and suspended at its outer end by two guys. I couldn't get a grip on the pole because the boat was rolling so much and I couldn't keep my balance. I dropped the mainsail to stop the boat moving, and then swung the pole around until it fetched up against the forestay. I adjusted the guys to keep it there and next tried to release the two levers which held it in its heel arrangement on the mast. This, for me, was physically the hardest piece of work on board. I had to hold the levers down and at the same time try and pull back the pole (which was twenty feet long) and all the while try to steady myself against the rolling motion. The wind by now had reached near gale force. After several attempts I eventually

freed the pole from its fitting and landed it safely on deck, but
the whole operation had taken an hour and a half and I was
physically exhausted. I went below, made a cup of hot chocolate
and firmly resolved to eat more spinach in future.

My day's run at noon the next day I measured as 170 miles
which was pretty good, but it didn't dispel the uneasiness I was
beginning to feel about my astro navigation. In fact I wasn't
sure that it didn't aggravate my doubts. For some while now my
sextant positions had been at variance with my dead-reckoning –
or where I thought I was; I wondered if my compass error
could be suspect. I got out my navigation books and worked
through some examples of how to determine compass error, and
it was then I discovered that I'd been making a monumental
blunder. I had been *adding* the magnetic variation to the compass error! Consequently, I had a total error of 59° west which
is probably the biggest on record.

Now, the above may sound as if I now knew what was going
on – in fact, I still had no idea. Rob had forgotten to tell me
that compass error was a *combination* of magnetic variation
and compass deviation. He obviously assumed I would know
this, but certain things don't appear as clearly to me as they do
to the rest of the human race.

My log recorded the breakthrough:

I feel in an exceptionally good temper at present having now
solved the problem of the compass error and its influence on
my weird positions. I won't go into details, suffice it to say
that those people who know me very well – and fortunately
there aren't many – will ask themselves how on earth a duffer
like me thinks she can navigate round the world when she
doesn't even know the difference between compass error and
deviation! If Rob had been here and witnessed this mental
struggle, his derision would have so deflated me that I should
never have found the solution at all, but would have continued
across the ocean in a series of zigzags, probably ending up in
Alaska.

I have this obsession about not wanting to appear stupid in

front of those whose opinion I esteem. I often feel that I am better off saying and doing nothing so that at least there remains an element of doubt.

By this time I was at 33° south and had altered course towards Cape Town. The days' runs were good, but I sensed that the weather was going to change. I was still north of the line of depressions but began to watch the barometer closely now for an indication of something new. I didn't have to wait very long.

At six o'clock in the morning of 3 November the kettle leapt off the stove and clattered its way noisily over the chart-table seat. I must have been sound asleep, for I was only aware of being rudely wakened and had no idea what caused the noise. I noticed the motion was unsteady so I jumped out of my bunk to look at the wind indicator. It read thirty to forty knots. I pulled on my boots and oilskins and went up on deck to find the telltale white caps and streaks of a full-blown westerly gale. I put an additional reef in the mainsail, and then went down below to write up my log. While I was sitting at the chart table a large wave picked *Crusader* up and threw her sideways. I dashed on deck to grab the wheel, but the self-steering gear was already bringing her back on course. I returned below and closed the hatch so the only signs of what was happening outside were the muffled whines of the wind and an occasional lurch.

During the afternoon the barometer fell another 4 millibars and the wind increased to forty knots plus. It looked as if I was going to get a chance to test all the improvements I'd been making. At 8.30 the wind was up to fifty knots at times, and I took down all sail except for the deep-reefed main. The barometer continued to drop during the morning, and I was feeling very apprehensive. At 2 a.m. I wrote:

Will this wind never cease? It is a constant fifty knots and waves are exploding against the coachroof and into the cockpit. Twice *Crusader* has been thrown off course and gybed. A short while ago I heard the roar of a breaking wave behind, but she must have surfed in front of it because only a small amount of water came into the cockpit. My heart was thudding like mad when the roaring stopped.

9 a.m. Still it goes on. The wind speed indicator is occasionally pressed hard against the stops at sixty knots and the wind makes yesterday's feel like a breeze! I had only an hour and a half's sleep last night but really don't feel so bad. I've been up on deck and considered taking down the mainsail, but it's kept me out of danger so far so I think I'll leave it. Unbelievably the Sailomat continues to hold a marvellous course most of the time and although the boat has been knocked over a few times never once has it reached a dangerous angle.

I seem to be waiting for the boat to capsize but perhaps that won't happen. I completed one more item of preparation this morning when I put a holding bolt on the cooker. I'm having to pump the bilges more now, and the first thing I intend doing when this gale blows itself out is to find where the water's coming from.

10 a.m. The barometer is rising very slowly. Crusader has just been caught in a confusion of cross seas, and the last one dealt her a mighty whack on the bow which knocked her bodily sideways. When I looked out of the window it seemed as if she was riding on a glacier of white foam. Come on, Crusader, show 'em what you're made of!

By 2 p.m. the worst was over, the wind began to fall below forty knots and the knot of anxiety in my stomach started to unwind itself. I made myself some breakfast. I felt lethargic and tired but happy that Crusader and I had both come through unscathed. I thought of all the hours I had sat, tense and apprehensive at the chart table, and smiled wryly to myself because my anxiety had been unnecessary. I wondered if I would react in the same way next time a severe gale developed.

I pondered, too, over the tactics I'd adopted and wasn't altogether happy with what I'd done. I'd treated the mainsail as a storm tri-sail and risked damaging the most important sail on board. It should have been taken down in forty knots of wind but I had it up in sixty! Well, I'd been lucky, and I'd also been very lucky with the self-steering gear. If I had decided to disengage the Sailomat and steer the boat myself then I should have been exhausted, because the gale lasted longer than I could have endured. And an exhausted crew unable to cope with unexpected emergencies is only one step from disaster. Besides it would have been very difficult to disengage the self-steering gear and stow it once the gale had really started. so in a way I had committed myself.

I have said that I was lucky in respect of these oversights, and lucky I was because they were not genuine oversights but neglect. I was reluctant – in fact frightened – to do anything I didn't really have to do. These conclusions didn't come to the surface, but I was aware of them just the same. I accepted them, subconsciously, as the truth. Had something happened which demanded my attention then I would have responded, helped by the urgency of the situation, and fear wouldn't have come into it. But to overcome that cold lethargy that crept over me while I *waited* for something to happen demanded a will-power which I wasn't certain that I had.

The passing of the gale left me with plenty to do. I thought, or hoped, that after this gale the wind would moderate, the sea become steady and that then I would be able to turn in and sleep. Unfortunately, that didn't happen as the extracts from my log for the 4th and 5th November show:

> This steep, wallowing motion is driving me insane. It's just the sort of sea that riles Rob, and he'd be swearing like mad if he were here. I'd feel better if I knew how much progress I have made, but I can't even take a sun-sight because the horizon is lost with this crazy movement. I've just stepped into the cockpit and put my foot in a bucket of water. I'm so fed up I'm going to bed.

It continues later:

> If a gale is frightening, then to the same degree, its aftermath is frustrating; at most I had two hours' sleep, and most of this time I was disturbed by the empty sails crashing in this cursed swell. At 4.30 I sheeted the genoa and the mainsail hard in, and tried to sleep, but the noise continued and by 6.00 I was defeated. There need to be twenty-five knots of wind to sail properly under these conditions and at present there are less than ten. I tried putting the wind just aft the

The chart table at which I worked, read and ate

Looking aft through the saloon towards the galley and chart area

Left: Trying to shoot the sun while balanced momentarily on the top of a wave

Right: My navigation was a bit shaky when I started but I learnt as I went along

Below: Crusader is showing her paces as she beats towards Cape Town

Overleaf: Leaving the shelter of the Falkland Islands to brave the last 1000 miles of the Southern Ocean

Left: Sunny, windy and cold

Below left: Sheeting in a headsail required a lot of effort but these self tailing winches made the job a lot easier

Below: Hundreds of large but friendly pilot whales shepherded me out of the Roaring Forties

Left: Working on the rigging repairs in Port Stanley

Above: My 'knitting' on the mast which held it up for 3000 miles

Left: Repairing sail damage was a boring task but fortunately it wasn't often necessary

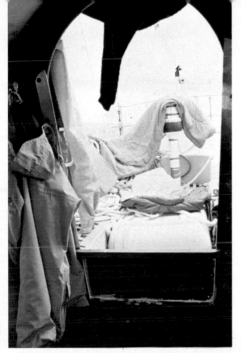

Left: Drying out after heavy weather

Checking sail trim

The evening sky promises
no storm for tomorrow

Above: Doing 8 knots in
a fresh breeze under
working sails

Right: Greeting Rob at
the last rendezvous

Overleaf: Five miles from the finish early on June the 18th

Above: Together after nine and a half months

Right: My family from New Zealand, Austria and England who gathered to welcome me home

Overleaf: Approaching the
Dartmouth Embankment at the end
of the voyage

beam to keep some wind in the sails and prevent them collapsing each time *Crusader* rolled, but it hasn't helped. The swells are twenty feet high and in their troughs there is no wind at all. I feel so useless I could scream.

9.00 a.m. I've taken down the genoa which was flogging uselessly, and I'm trying to keep the main full, no matter what direction I'm headed. I'm also afraid that the Sailomat might be damaged by the pounding of water under the transom as she pitches. When I'm up on deck I find it helps to yell loudly at the sea birds. However, they appear remarkably impervious to my uncomplimentary remarks. A big fat albatross just flew past and gave me a close look, then plonked himself down in the wake and eyed me expectantly – I think not for insults but rather for something to eat. With his big feet flapping he could keep up with me quite easily. Stupid-looking thing!

Later on, however, I was feeling a little more composed:

I'm feeling quite pleased with my efforts this morning. I had given up sailing as a bad job and had tried to find out how all that water was getting in during the gale. It meant pouring buckets of water over the deck and diving quickly into lockers to see if I could see anything dripping. I suspected it could have been a leak from one of the cockpit drains, but Andrew had done a marvellous job, and they all looked in excellent condition. Eventually, I found a hole in the deck through which the stern-light cable ran. I decided that could account for a lot of the water and, as the stern-light didn't work anyway, I filled in the hole with a wooden bung and some Plastic Padding. I also took the mainsail down because it was flogging and getting on my nerves. Then I repaired a seam along one of the battens and re-stitched a slide fastening. Finally, I tightened the bottle screws on the upper and lower shrouds and dropped my large screwdriver overboard. It was a nice one, too, with a red handle. I hate losing things anyway but especially like this; it reminds me of the finality at the edge of the boat.

While I was tightening the rigging I noticed an incredible number of barnacles beneath the boat's waterline, some of them were two inches long! They were revolting-looking things, and

when I pulled one off it felt positively alive. They were even
growing on the Sailomat oar and rudder. How the evil little
things managed to hang on and grow at the speed we were going
I simply couldn't imagine. On the evening of the 5th, in my
'happy hour' (the regular time each day set aside for crews to
relax and have a tot of rum), I re-read bits of Chay's book and
noted in my log:

> I'm reading *The Impossible Voyage*, and I'm amused to see
> how much Chay and I differ, especially in our concern for the
> welfare of loved ones. Of course his situation was a lot
> different from mine because he had a wife and a baby to
> consider. Perhaps I'm a natural loner because as long as I
> know that Rob is alive and well I don't really worry about
> him. He has his life to live and I've got mine, and if I can
> survive then I'm sure he can. He may worry about me, but
> that is a condition to which he has been reconciled right from
> the beginning, and the reverse is true for me. Again, unlike
> Chay, I rarely listen to the news; and when I do listen it
> doesn't concern me deeply. I live my own life, and I'd prefer
> the rest of the world to live theirs. Another difference
> between Chay and myself is that he is moderately religious
> whereas I am not. He said I would change my mind about
> religion before the end of the voyage, but I can't imagine it. If
> he means that survival is a matter of faith then I'll agree with
> him, but on rather different terms. I have to laugh at some of
> his anecdotes – what it is to have a good sense of humour!

I appreciated Chay's sense of humour very much and was
always looking for things to laugh at whether in books or over
the radio. Boris had made me laugh and I talked to him at
times, surprising myself with the sound of my own voice. For
ages after he'd gone I hardly ever spoke aloud. Then I suddenly
remembered the rendezvous in a couple of weeks' time and
thought that if I didn't get some practice I might lose my voice.
I didn't want to talk to myself (in case I thought I was going
nutty!) but memorized the songs of Olivia Newton-John and
Edith Piaf and sung them to the birds and the ocean.

7 November (Day 60) and trouble.

Well! Surprise, surprise! I've looked at the self-steering and find I have another broken rudder! At first I stared at it in amazement. The shaft, made of quarter-inch walled aluminium tube, had broken in two. I wonder whatever caused that to happen? It must have collided with something.

It took me five hours to repair it and during that time I didn't once have to touch the helm. *Crusader*, I discovered, was so beautifully balanced under jib, staysail and main that on some points of sailing I obviously didn't need self-steering anyway.

Although I hadn't officially reached the Southern Ocean, I was far enough south to be affected by its weather. It had already become cold enough for me to change into winter clothes. I had lots of good new woolly stuff which was fun to put on for the first time, though it was less appealing after four and a half months!

Occasionally I would switch on the radio telephone receiver (the only part that was working) and tune to the Portishead frequency. Invariably I heard conversations between sailor husbands and wives which made me feel rather lonely. I did think of listening during the hours I was supposed to report to the *Daily Express*, but there was really no point. I didn't want to hear anyone calling when I couldn't answer; besides, it used up the batteries.

On 8 November, Day 61, I realized I had made a mistake in a noon-sight which I had taken three days earlier and wasn't as far south as I imagined. That mistake cost me at least three days' progress because I had drifted into the high pressure zone and lost the wind. Fog appeared, too, with clouds moving low over the water and looking distressingly like land. It made me wonder if my navigation was really haywire and whether I was about to make a landfall in Namibia! But if I was worried about landfalls on that occasion it was nothing to the paroxysms of uncertainty I was to suffer a week later, when after three successive and splendid days' runs, I wrote in my log:

> I am either nowhere near South Africa or else I'm about to trip over it in the dark! After 6000 miles of ocean I'm very

nervous about approaching land. I've taken lots of sights which all put me in the same place, but I can't get rid of the sense of insecurity. How peaceful the last weeks appear now, with the thought of what the next few days will bring. I wish I could continue on my way without having to go close to the land for the rendezvous.

To take my mind off the worry I wrote letters and finished the article I was writing for the *Daily Express*. In the evenings I worked on my chess pieces, and was quite pleased with the first knight, except that in my clumsiness I broke off both his sword and his nose and had to glue them back on.

18 November (Day 71) Disaster!

The Sailomat has suffered some irreparable damage due to continual waves hitting the stern, and I shall have to call into Cape Town to have it fixed.

It is a horrible decision to have to make, but to continue without adequate self-steering would be stupid at this stage. I should be thankful that it's happened now and not a week after Cape Town. I feel so depressed – the fact that I'll be able to have a bath and eat a steak doesn't impress me at all. I can spend the rest of my life having baths, and would much rather be moving on even though it means being out in the cold Southern Ocean. If only I had brought some more bolts with me . . ., but one can't remember everything. Well, there's no point in moping – just accept the fact and do what has to be done.

I'm running almost parallel with the shore but fifty miles off, heading for Table Bay where I hope to pick up a pilot to guide me in. I've got charts of the coast but none of the harbours.

I think I can see a light patch in the sky above the place where Cape Town should be; I wish it was daylight so that I could be certain. I've spent hours these past two days reading details of the coastline, but without detailed charts I wouldn't dare to risk closing the land during darkness.

The next morning I wrote:

Land! That bright patch in the sky *was* Cape Town. I can see lots of ships heading there. And now with the daybreak I can see Table Mountain and what the Pilot book calls 'The Twelve Apostles'. I hardly dare believe it!

9

THREE DAYS IN CAPE TOWN

I felt quite content as I sat on the stern and watched the mountains getting larger, and I wondered how quickly I'd be able to have the repairs done and be on my way again. I decided that three days was the limit: I just couldn't afford any more time and feel confident about getting round the Horn in decent weather.

Port Control told me that a warship would meet me outside the harbour and guide me in. Sure enough, as I approached Robben Island, I saw a minesweeper coming towards me. As she approached I dipped my ensign (although I wasn't altogether sure if it was the right thing to do), and I was happy to see that she did the same. They gave me a cheering welcome which I thought very kind. Then the captain congratulated me on my effort and sent over a chart of the harbour entrance; a second warship came up to say hello and sent over a few bottles of beer! Just short of the entrance they turned away and left me in the hands of two very impressive-looking tugs which came steaming out to show me the way in.

The rendezvous boat also arrived, and I explained that I had to stop for repairs. A woman reporter who was on board asked me if I was glad to see people again, and I'm afraid I pulled a face.

We proceeded into the yacht basin where, much to my surprise, there were lots of people on the quay. I motored slowly alongside the pontoon; a dozen hands reached out and made *Crusader* fast. (Evidently my silence those past six weeks had caused concern; ships had even been alerted to look out for me.)

Some of my helpers included a contingent from the Royal Cape Yacht Club, against whose pontoon I was moored, and the rear- and vice-commodores who welcomed me to CapeTown. After introductions they began to discuss what repairs I needed to have done. Rob had told me of Cape Town's helpfulness and hospitality, but this was incredible; *everyone* wanted to help! One local yachtsman, Jerry Whitehead, very kindly offered to see to the repairs to the Sailomat and promised it would be ready within two days. A reporter said he would call the *Daily Express* in London and get the news of my arrival passed on to my family. Then I was invited to the yacht club for a marvellous lunch. I found I wasn't able to eat as much as I had been used to at home; I think my stomach must have shrunk. I found it very strange to be sitting at a table again talking and listening to people; it felt abstract and unreal as if I wasn't really there at all. I could still feel the motion of *Crusader* under my feet, and the floor of the restaurant felt very hard and blunt, almost as if it was striking my feet when I walked.

I was invited by at least half a dozen people to stay at their homes, but I politely declined and explained that it would be best for me to stay on the boat. I didn't want to relax completely, fearing I might lose the rapport I had with *Crusader* and the sea. However, I did accept the invitation to dinner that night and the promise of a hot bath.

Unfortunately I had arrived on a Saturday and, as it was the week-end, none of the major repairs could be done. Consequently, I spent the rest of the day doing things myself, things which were easier to do at port than at sea; jobs such as checking the halyards for signs of chafe at the mast head etc. Two young locals, David Alcock and Ian Carter, came aboard and very kindly greased the winches and tightened the rudder post gland. In fact, lots of people came down to say hello and welcome me to Cape Town. I was overwhelmed by their friendliness and genuine desire to do any little thing that would help me get shipshape again. Many of them said they'd talked to Rob – the surest way of getting my avid attention!

There were lots of reporters and photographers who all wanted to know how things had gone over the last weeks, and by the time I'd finished talking to them Bill O'Reilly, a member of the Royal Cape Yacht Club, had come to collect me for my hot bath and barbecue. I took the bunch of letters the Cape Town newspaper, *Argus*, had for me and, while being driven by Bill O'Reilly to his family house in the hills overlooking Cape Town, I thought with pleasure of reading all the news from home.

That evening as soon as we arrived at Bill's house (not wanting to appear over-anxious!) I dived into a bath full to the brim with hot soapy water and smelling of all the beautiful things I'd forgotten over the last nine weeks. It was unbelievably good.

Later, feeling relaxed, I read my mail and tried to ring Juliet, realizing from her letters how worried she was by my silence. Unfortunately, she wasn't at home, but I was able to contact my parents-in-law, who were obviously delighted to hear from me. They had already heard of my arrival and had phoned Juliet in Vienna. The *Daily Express*, I was relieved to hear, had called my parents in New Zealand; poor things, they must have been frantic. Everyone was well, and Rob was expected in Auckland on 26 November. Sadly he wouldn't know until then about my arrival in Cape Town as he was not in direct radio contact.

After dinner my hosts drove me down to the harbour; I thanked them for a lovely evening and went to bed, but not to sleep, unfortunately, because after nine weeks of noise and movement I found the still and quiet of being in harbour curiously disturbing. I lay awake worrying about the repairs, about Rob and the bother I had caused the family. I consoled myself with the thought that at least my family would have learnt that silence doesn't necessarily mean disaster. But the long-term worry I was giving them was nevertheless the most unpalatable aspect of the voyage. Rob and I had both agreed that it was right for me to attempt to sail round the world and we thought I would be justified in the end, but I was always conscious that I was causing them immense worry, and when I read their letters it nagged me again that I was being very selfish and unkind. However, it had to be, and anyone making this sort of journey must be a little hard-hearted.

There was no profit in going over the same old questions. I had committed myself and everyone else to this venture, and the only way I could justify having started was to carry on and finish it – to get it over as soon as possible and to make damn sure I got back in one piece.

Early on the morning of the 20th (Day 72) the radio repairman arrived and diagnosed the fault – a blown fuse! The silly thing was that, although I had changed all the fuses several times, all my spare fuses were blown too. Evidently, as the repairman later discovered, the real trouble was a crack in the aerial insulator.

Cape Town hospitality knew no bounds. The manager of the President Hotel called to collect my laundry and delivered it the next evening wrapped up like a Christmas present; it was marvellous to have clean, sweet-smelling clothes again. Then my winch-greasing friends returned with Jerry Whitehead, who offered to let me use a little of his time on the slipway. We had *Crusader* slipped and they helped me scrub off the barnacles and touch up the bottom of the boat with anti-fouling. Then the radio man arrived with the new insulator and it occurred to me that the gifts I had received – two crates of port and one crate of sherry – were one thing, but that I must be running up quite a bill over my other acquisitions.

The embarrassing thing was that I had brought no money with me, other than the ten-pound note Juliet had insisted I take in case I landed on some strange shore with nothing except the clothes on my back. Fortunately the *Argus* came to my aid and supplied me with money which was to be reimbursed by the *Daily Express*. Due to everyone's kindness I hardly needed any. I didn't need much food as I still had about ten months' supply on board, but I was getting tired of my collection of cassettes, so I bought a couple more. I also bought a few more books and the kind man in the bookshop gave me one as a present.

I bought myself another track suit, as I'd found them more comfortable to wear than jeans. I also spotted a pair of pyjamas and thought how nice it would be to change out of my polar suit occasionally and wear pyjamas in bed. That evening I had a delightful dinner with David Alcock and his family and listened to some views on South Africa and its problems.

By Monday, late afternoon, almost everything was complete,

and *Crusader* was resting snugly against the pontoon waiting for her departure. She looked clean and spruce and, I thought, very businesslike. She looked the part somehow, not as if she were a cruising boat off for a day's sailing or a flashy racer, but lean and purposeful and ready to take on anything. I hardly ever saw her from a spectator's vantage point, and my judgement may have been biased; it was difficult to be objective!

I was due to leave the following day, but the spare rudder shafts of the self-steering gear still had to be made – the firm had promised to work on them all night. I spent the evening with Ian Carter's family who own a beautiful house in the Cape Town suburbs; the most attractive thing about the house for me, perhaps understandably, was the size of the bath, and I spent a delicious half-hour trying to soak up enough perfume and suds to last me for another six to seven months. The dinner was fantastic, and I dwelt over the flavour of roast meat and vegetables; nothing had ever tasted so good. I was taken back to the boat again and one of the company, who was an electrician, tried to repair my off-course alarm. He discovered a fault and replaced a part, but I had no repair manual for these complex instruments and eventually he had to admit defeat.

I got into bed and had almost dropped off when I heard a voice calling from the pier. I emerged to find an elderly Dutch gentleman to whom I'd spoken earlier. He was laden to the hilt with all sorts of goodies he thought I might find useful: a bag of oranges, an old atlas, a small hand-bearing compass, a thermos water bottle, a torch, a bottle of ginger beer, an inflatable pillow and two bottles of wine. I was very touched by his generosity and the trouble he had taken to bring them. He wandered off again down the quay looking happy and disappeared into the night. Pleased but puzzled I climbed back into my bunk and wondered what had prompted him to come down so late at night to give me these things. There are people in the world who will go to extraordinary lengths to help; perhaps they can relate in a personal way to a strange and seemingly mad venture such as this. I felt I knew what it meant to him to give me these treasures, which, in a survival situation, are exactly what I would need. I added the thermos flask, the inflatable pillow and the hand-bearing compass to my survival kit and often remembered the pleasure and excitement on his face as he produced them one after another from his bag.

Bright and early on Tuesday morning I made a mad dash into town with the Alcocks to get some fresh fruit and vegetables from the market. I returned and, while waiting for the promised self-steering parts to arrive, I changed my fresh-water supply, as it tended to grow algae even in a relatively short time. I'd found earlier a leak in one of the main tanks and tightened a wet hose connection. It wouldn't have been a disaster if the tank had drained because I had seventy-five gallons in reserve, but it would have meant having to collect water every time it rained.

I had just finished washing the decks and tidying up when the new shafts arrived, and I quickly reassembled the gear. I didn't know how to thank the people who had worked so hard and long to make them.

Then I very nearly blotted my copybook by attempting to leave Cape Town without clearing Customs. Fortunately, I was reminded in time and visited the various offices to complete required formalities. I called into the yacht club on the way back to the harbour to thank them for their hospitality. Then I was back on board and anxious to get off. When the moment came I had some difficulty in clearing the berth, clouted a post and wondered how on earth Rob had managed on *Great Britain II* when he called in there.

After much shuffling and pulling and help from ashore, we got the bow round and I cleared the forward pontoon by a matter of inches. Now I *was* off, motoring slowly between the boats and out of the yacht basin. With tears in my eyes I waved to all the people who had helped me so much. Their shouts of good-bye and good luck were drowned by the yacht club's loudspeaker and hoots from neighbouring boats. As I motored away I felt relief, not apprehension at the thought of the next four and a half months in the Roaring Forties – relief because I was on my way again and the journey was once more a reality.

10
INTO THE ROARING FORTIES

The wind was blowing hard by the time I cleared the harbour. I put on my oilskins and hoisted the No. 2 yankee and reefed the mainsail. I was busy trimming the sails when I realized I hadn't noted which side of the entrance buoy I was supposed to go. I rushed below and looked at the chart; to my horror I saw I was on the wrong side. The soles of my feet tickled as I waited for the rocks to claw at *Crusader*'s hull, but there was evidently plenty of water, and she glided smoothly over the rippled surface and on into the bay. I did, however, make certain this time to pass Robben Island on the right side – the short side, which saved me about five miles.

I laid a course to clear Sea Point and began to make good progress. But the strong wind I had experienced immediately outside the harbour began to drop away and by the time I was a mile or so offshore it had practically gone altogether. By 3 p.m. I was totally becalmed and about to endure the two most tedious and exhausting nights and days of the trip. The wind came and went repeatedly in the most exasperating fashion; I'd make a few miles, then lose the wind and drift back with the current. The place was notorious for its storms, but for me it couldn't rustle up as much as a steady force two! And I thought I'd never see the last of Table Mountain. Twenty hours after leaving the harbour I was only twenty miles west of the shore lights with the lights of the ships all round me. I drank endless mugs of cocoa and listened to my cassettes. It was quite impossible to sleep with the land so close and with what little wind there was doing its best to drive me on to the rocks.

23 November (Day 76)

I switched on my VHF and to my surprise heard Cape Town Radio calling me. There was a report that *Condor* was due in to Auckland on Thursday and *Great Britain II* the following day. I would rather have heard it the other way round, but it was great news anyway. It means I shall be able to talk to Rob again soon. What a surprise he's going to get!

I was equally surprised how easy it was to slip back into my old routine, and it soon felt as if I had never called in at Cape Town. As usual I was impatiently trying to hurry away from land, but in these hopeless winds I was making no progress and simply exhausting myself with needless sail changes. Where were all those gales?!

When the wind finally did return it immediately broke one of my new self-steering rudders. I could hardly believe it, and I felt so depressed I could have wept. How could the rudder have broken so easily? After all, the wind hadn't been *that* strong. For a while I considered turning back to Cape Town, but then I thought over the problem and estimated that would mean a possible eight- or nine-day delay. Such delay might make all the difference between late summer and autumn at the Horn, and heaven knows I was late enough already. I simply couldn't risk any more delay and was determined to continue. I still had two spare rudders below, plus an old one which I had shortened. I decided to risk it and hoped that whatever strange factors contributed to the breakage (hitting a wave at an unfortunate angle, or some inherent flaw in the metal) would not occur again. I also decided to cable Sailomat in Sweden to ask them if they could send out another rudder to my next rendezvous in Tasmania. Meanwhile, I still had the broken rudder to repair and this turned out to be a real schermozzle. I also got the damned halyard stuck again and felt so weary at the end of it all that I didn't have the energy to take off my sea boots before going to bed.

Later on the 25th I added in my log:

I've read all my letters again and Rob's log for the third time. The letters are all very encouraging, and if I ever feel unable to make the effort I'll just read them again! There seem to be a lot of people putting world maps on their walls showing my position, and I must produce some progress for them. I'm going to have a cup of cocoa now and go to bed – it's 8 p.m. – and I've set the alarm for midnight to make the call to Rob. Thinking about it, if this rudder lasts a week and a bit and the others a similar time, then assuming I can repair them with the new supply of bolts, they should last me up to my rendezvous in Tasmania – especially if I do some steering myself in the rough weather. I wish I didn't feel so nervous. It's the thought of the Roaring Forties, I suppose.

After three days I was not very far from Cape Town, but at least clear of the shallow Aghullus Bank which had given Chay such a frightful time on his first attempt alone around the world. He was in a little bilge keel boat, totally unsuitable for the journey, and while crossing the Aghullus Bank he was knocked flat eleven times. He had no alternative but to give up, and it clearly was a terrific disappointment. Even on his second attempt on *British Steel* he'd been plagued by squalls and gales in this very corner which was treating me so kindly. I suppose I shouldn't have complained.

The next morning, on 26 November, my log records:

Spoke to Rob! I switched on just before midnight as per schedule and Cape Town Radio was already calling me. They're on the ball. They put me straight through and there he was! My dear darling Rob. He sounded rather muffled as though he was talking through a shell, but quite loud.

He had a fantastic race to Auckland, faster than hoped. He has not received my letters yet but expects them any day now. He had been dying to know all the details, but of course I was more interested in hearing him talk!

We chatted for twenty-seven minutes. It was so great to hear him. Before his arrival in New Zealand all his crew were making jokes about irate in-laws waiting on the quay with shotguns, and he sounded rather nervous about meeting them. He also told me that they'd had only one gale since leaving England! Incredible. That makes me feel immeasurably better.

After talking to Rob, home seemed so much closer. I was about 7000 miles from him, but as he was staying in Auckland for a month I thought I should be able to catch up about 3500 miles on him. Moreover, I wouldn't be calling at Auckland, so that should enable me to make up an additional 500 miles. On the other hand I would lose this advantage across the Southern Ocean because my track would be further north and longer than that followed by the racing yachts. Rob warned me again on the radio about the danger of trying to save mileage by sailing further south and thus closer to the great circle track. He said it was too cold, much too hard work and altogether too dangerous for a single-hander. The greatest dangers were ice and icebergs. Racing yachts are able to watch out for them because they have large crews, but for a lone person the danger is immense. As much as I wanted to get round the Horn as quickly as possible it would have been fatal for me to consider tangling with icebergs – even if I could have survived the below-zero temperatures, the snow and iced-up decks. The difference in mileage between my proposed route and that which the majority of racing yachts took from Cape Town to the Horn (including the extra hop to Auckland) was over 2000 miles, but it couldn't be helped – I had to stay with the longer route and hope there were no icebergs further north than 48°, the approximate summer limit. I had never seen an iceberg and I didn't particularly want to!

27 November (Day 80)
I am now five days out of Cape Town and the wind is still spasmodic. I have set a SE course to head to the southern limit of my planned route, where I hope to pick up steadier winds.

I steered for a couple of hours last night and again this following morning, but while the speed remains below six knots I reckon the self-steering will hold together. I hate steering and know now that this is one of the major causes of my uneasiness. The prospect of having to steer eight to ten hours a day is horrible and boring in the extreme.

28 November, 6 p.m. (Day 81)
I've been steering on and off all day and reading the *Antarctic Pilot* in between. What an interesting book! Not only does it give information on all the local nasties but also lots of stuff on birds, fish, kelp and so on. Also, for psychological reasons, I've fished out Robin Knox-Johnson's

and Chichester's books again, and I'm reading what they have written about this part of the ocean. I find it helps to read about their troubles. *Crusader* is rolling quite heavily, and my glass of sherry has neatly deposited its contents on to the floor, so I've helped myself to some more.

At 11.30 p.m. I wrote:

The wind reached gale force at 8 p.m., and I have been on the wheel or changing sail ever since. At one point while going forward to hoist the storm jib the boat accidentally gybed, and by the time I got back to the wheel to bring her around she was hard into the wind and would neither tack nor gybe; the wind was really howling and I was sure that something would break. I turned the wheel hard over, disconnected the self-steering and rushed forward to haul down the mainsail. Halfway down it wrapped itself around the mast and stuck like glue. I ran back to the cockpit and threw the wheel hard over the opposite way to gybe and free the sail from the mast. It did the trick; I hauled the sail down as quickly as I could and lashed it to the boom. I didn't want to stay lying-a-hull with no sail hoisted, because the waves were too big already, so I hoisted the storm jib (the size of a large tablecloth) and turned down wind again. What a performance!

The following afternoon, I wrote:

The wind's dying at last. At 23.00 last night the barometer started to rise from 1008 mlb and reached 1023 mlb this morning. The wind continued to howl through the night and I had no sleep till about 05.00, although I have been sleeping on and off all morning. I was immensely relieved to find I didn't have to steer during the gale as I discovered; with the storm jib sheeted flat fore and aft, *Crusader* kept a perfect course downwind without the aid of the Sailomat. Early this morning, I cooked myself a large breakfast of fried potatoes, pumpkin and eggs and although I was feeling a little sick – due to tiredness I expect – I ate it and went back to bed. Two hours ago the wind and sea began to ease. I was due to cross the 40th parallel in the night but with the wind backing and driving me north I'm probably back on 39° somewhere.

Suddenly it is very cold. I have changed into a polar suit with a shirt underneath, a track suit, socks and wool-lined

slippers. I feel very snug. Outside it is bleak in the extreme.
A grey lumpy sea, grey sky and the odd wandering albatross
cruising in between the waves.

I had been very puzzled the day before to notice that the
barometer kept jumping 3 millibars. Then I discovered the
reason; I was banging my head on it! I had hung it up above the
saloon doorway and thought its base was well out of the way,
but I must be taller than I thought I was.

Every time I look into the saloon I'm confronted by a large,
snowy Christmas cake with marzipan toadstools on it which
was given to me by the *Argus* in Cape Town. I'm in a
quandary as to what to do; it's too big to go in any lockers,
and it's too beautiful to throw away, but if I don't move the
cake it's going to end up in the bilges. It's got a big
gingerbread house and reminds me of the picture books I
read as a child. I think that for Christmas Day I shall cut a
slice off which includes the house and sacrifice the remainder.
It will give the birds a treat, anyway.

I hadn't been able to take any sights for two days because of
the overcast skies, but it didn't really matter. There was absolutely nothing to bang into. Now that I knew there were no
islands or ships about I stopped watching out for them.

However, the next morning after breakfast I decided I really
ought to try and take a sight. Measuring the sun's altitude can
be a funny experience on a yacht in heavy seas. Not only do you
have to hold the sextant with both hands, keep the spray off the
mirrors and somehow try to hang on, but there is also the problem of knowing when the horizon *is* the horizon, or if you're
staring at a wave twenty yards off. When looking through the
instrument's telescope it is extremely hard to decide, especially
when you only have a second or so in which to make up your
mind. The whole business is also aggravated by the necessity of
having to hold notepaper against the wind, clench a pencil in
your teeth and keep and eye on the chronometer! By the time
I'd taken five sights, I was feeling pretty pleased with myself.

I then plotted the sights and discovered to my disgust that the
last days' runs were not anything like as good as I had thought
they would be. The current must still have been running against

me. I was also disappointed to discover I had been pushed north; this was half expected, but I had not imagined myself to be as far north as 38°51'. Fortunately, the wind had now eased and steadied so I was able to keep a good course to the SE. The speed was good but too much for the self-steering. To avoid damage I disconnected it and settled myself behind the wheel. I was prepared to steer for the rest of the day, but then I noticed that *Crusader* was doing very nicely on her own. I'd forgotten that this was her best point of balance, with the mainsail reefed, a working jib and the staysail set. For the rest of the day she pounded contentedly over the big seas at seven knots, occasionally being thrown by a big wave but always coming back on to course by herself, and I didn't touch the wheel once. This was very encouraging because it meant if the self-steering broke down altogether, at least I would have some break from steering.

The weather was much as I had expected, with sudden gales that would last for days and then drop away to nothing, leaving *Crusader* to flounder in the oily swells like a dying duck. Rob had given me some good lessons on the weather patterns here, and I knew that the weather I was getting was caused by depressions moving along to the south of me. These depressions follow a well-beaten track from the west, and they moan their way along those vast, empty stretches of ocean with virtually no land in their way to impede them. This endless, circulating passage of strong winds and the subsequent shifts that come with depressions create the phenomenal freak waves, or 'grey beards', as the old sailing ship men used to call them. The waves they told stories about I couldn't even bear to think about. Francis Chichester wrote a super book called, *Along the Clipper Way*, which describes some of the hair-raising experiences of the old Clipper ships; there were also fabulous stories of giant squids rising up out of the sea and drawing whole ships down into the depths. . . .

Fortunately, my imagination stopped short of any squid more than a few inches long, but the idea of waves big enough to swamp large ships worried me, as my log on 1st December showed:

After hoisting the reefed main again I spent a long time standing by the wheel, watching the boat's progress and thinking: to port lies sunshine, to starboard lie polar bears, burrr! (Of course there aren't any but it feels as though there should be.) All day I've been trying to come to terms with the fact that I feel nervous, but really it's not surprising. People talk about grey-bearders, freak waves and the rest, and behind every ripple I expect to see a mile-high wave lurking! At present there's a twenty-foot swell running. But I have to stick it out even if old Neptune himself tells me to clear out. This is the nitty-gritty of the journey so far as my survival's concerned; this is what it is all about and naturally I'm nervous when I think of the dire things that could happen. But then standing here at the wheel and watching *Crusader* weave down the waves, I think to myself; surely a boat is like a cork and as long as she's got strong sides and lots of air in the middle she'll float even if she's turned upside down. The mast is the most vulnerable part; obviously I have to try and stay upright.

On re-reading, this account sounds flippant but, in fact, I am really very anxious, and flippancy is my guard against being morbid. Darling Rob, I wish I was homeward-bound already. You've suggested I shouldn't worry about speed but should just plod along. OK, I'll try very hard just to *plod* when I next meet a force ten.

Talking to Rob again today was odd in some ways. He was close enough to be reached by phone but not close enough to help me – other than to give encouragement and moral strength. In the half dozen times I have talked to him in Auckland he has made a tremendous difference to my state of mind; he made me feel less afraid of the weather and has altogether put me in great spirits, despite the almost continuous near gales I have experienced. In fact, I now find these gales preferable to the light and irritating variable winds of the tropics.

Talking to Rob has also made the days hurry by, and they've been more meaningful and not just time passed unnoticed.

Local time in New Zealand is eight hours ahead of me, so I have to be considerate in my choice of radio link times, otherwise poor Rob would have to get out of bed in the early hours of the morning. Of course to suit him *I* have to get out

of bed in the early hours, but, then, as getting up in the night
is routine with me, it really doesn't matter.

7 December (Day 90)
Today is so incredibly beautiful that I've vacated the cabin
and am sitting in the sun marvelling at how the Southern
Ocean can turn on such weather. There has been no strong
wind for the past three days and the sea is almost flat, even
the swell has almost gone. The only wind is a gentle and steady
breeze from the east which means I'm close hauled heading SE.

Two things have puzzled me this morning. The first was a
series of long lines of foam on the water as if a ship had
recently passed, but that is unlikely. The second is that it
looks as though my noon to noon run has exceeded 200 miles,
which is unbelievable, because I haven't been averaging nine
knots, which is what this distance implies – it has been more
like seven knots. Perhaps the extra miles are due to the current.
I've checked and rechecked my morning sights and I'm sure
they're right, but it won't be until I take the noon-sight that I'll
know *exactly* how many miles I have covered. I suppose it *is*
possible to have a two-knot current? I can only conclude that it
must be so. Perhaps Rob will know when I call him tomorrow.

There are five different kinds of birds about the yacht; one
little grey thing keeps threatening to land on the mast but
hasn't yet dared. Poor thing, the Southern Ocean is no place
to be if you're likely to get tired!

The wake is a straight line of bubbles stretching into the
distance, and *Crusader* is heeling gently under full sail,
ticking off the miles at a steady six knots. The air is cool, the
sea is cold but the sun from where I am sitting in the cockpit,
is hot enough to burn. Chasing around in my head are silly
doubts that I am not really here at all but in some tropical
latitude. I look for the characteristics to confirm the facts
but they simply aren't there. I have the sextant beside me now
and I mean to get my position right at lunchtime.

Characteristics came in plenty on 8 December, the following
day, when it blew a gale once more. I had disconnected the self-
steering in the afternoon because *Crusader* seemed happy to
steer by herself, but by 11 p.m. I was out of bed reconnecting it

again to control the crazy course she was making. By 2 a.m. the wind was up to forty knots so I altered course to bring it on the quarter. This was considerably more comfortable than having the wind on the beam, and with the No. 2 yankee up I was making six knots which meant another good day's run, albeit more to the south than I should have wished.

I really seemed to be streaking across the chart with these following winds; the Southern Ocean has its compensations. Nevertheless I should have been less optimistic and more mistrustful of the progress I was making, but out there, thousands of miles from land, I wasn't worried about navigation – just a little puzzled at the continued discrepancy between the distance obtained from my sights and those from the automatic log reading. I knew my sights must be right because I'd found the Canaries and Cape Town – but still . . . I must have been doing *something* wrong; I was sure Rob would be able to tell me.

10 December (Day 93)
It's been force seven all-day and the barometer is falling all the time; I wonder if it's because I'm moving south and closer to the depression. The motion of the boat is horrible. She's rolling heavily, and it has been impossible to relax in any position. This, combined with the falling glass, culminated in a small personal depression this afternoon. I was lying in my bunk finishing a book and became quite upset at the ending – something that very seldom happens. Then suddenly I asked myself what I thought I was doing here instead of being with Rob. After some more morbid thoughts and a little weep I jumped out of my bunk, made a cup of tea and read a page or two of Chichester's book to remind myself that it's not supposed to be all roses.

12 December, 15.30 (Day 95)
Crusader is cavorting down the waves like a fat lady after a very boisterous party, dipping her lee rail under the waves and occasionally taking a wave right over the deck. A short while ago all I could see from the cabin window was green water, quite a lot of which found its way down my neck! These windows will take a moderate amount of spray and rain

without leaking too badly but they object to total immersion. Water has also found its way through the cockpit, but again I can't see where. It's a nuisance although easily pumped out. Cooking is a real schermozzle; nothing stays where it's put no matter how well lodged. When I eat, one hand holds my cup, the other manoeuvres food into my mouth, still another holds the plate and the remainder keep me wedged into my seat. I'm learning to be an octopus. However, I feel quite cheerful and philosophical about this way of life; I suppose I'm getting used to it, and just as well.

13 December (Day 96)
What a hellish night! The wind increased to gale force again and with the wind on the beam *Crusader* was thrown about like a cork. Several times I woke up in a panic as a wave broke on the deck overhead to send water cascading into the cockpit; I had to pump out the bilges continually. I thought I had stopped most of the leaks but water still gets in. Despite resolutions not to worry I lay in my bunk, tense, waiting for the next big wave and wondering if it would smash the self-steering.

14 December (Day 97)
What a Charlie I am! ! ! I called Rob this morning, explained the discrepancies I was getting and discovered I had been making a monumental blunder. Instead of measuring the distances on the latitude scale at the side of the chart, I had been measuring them on the longitude scale along the bottom! Rob figured it out immediately; I suppose almost anyone but me would have solved the problem.

So *that* explains the phenomenal current of two knots that carried me an extra forty miles or so a day. A great feeling while it lasted. I had to laugh at myself, me the big-shot navigator! It's a wonder I have managed to come this far. . . . Still, if I've succeeded in getting here as an idiot, perhaps I'll survive the whole journey as one.

Since calling Rob I have spent almost the entire morning trying to work out the *exact* mileage I have covered. I make it about 10,573 miles at an average day's run of 113.4 miles (I think). I'm feeling rather demoralized at the moment.

11
A LONELY CHRISTMAS

The weather continued cold, wet and nasty. A little after mid-night on the 18th I got up to try and call my parents in New Zealand. Unfortunately Cape Town Radio couldn't hear me, although I could just hear them calling me. It was blowing hard, and I was worried about the self-steering gear. It was really coping marvellously, but there was a limit to what I could expect it to stand up to. I had had to steer all of the previous day but managed to make things easier for myself by fitting the emergency tiller. It meant I didn't have to steer from the exposed aft end of the cockpit. Using a system of block and tackles led through the main hatch I could just manage to alter course without leaving the cabin. Even down wind *Crusader* would stay on course for quite a long time, and when she did sheer away it only needed a heave on the tiller to steady her again.

When I eventually got my telephone link call to New Zealand the reception was so bad that it was five minutes before I realized that the voice I could hear was Mother! Rob was stay-ing with my parents for a few days, but at that moment was in the pub with my father and brother. I yelled down the phone that I'd call again in the evening but didn't know whether Mother heard me. By the time I finally got through again it was three o'clock in the morning. The reception was bad again, but Rob and I were able to get across our usual questions, and we arranged another schedule for a few days later.

While waiting for my turn I had used the time to make a new self-steering rudder from the broken ones. (Another had snapped a few days previously.) The effort of trying to do this and pre-vent myself from being hurled from one end of the boat to the other was exhausting.

Next morning I wrote in my log:

I couldn't decide what to eat for breakfast this morning so
cooked lunch instead. I boiled some pasta and ended up with
a risotto of onion, peas and bacon grill, nice but a bit salty. I
had one sip from my cup of tea before it hit the floor. It's a
good thing I'm not inclined to bouts of temper or I'd have
gone batty by now. Even so, the odd nasty word does escape
my lips, I must admit.

The extreme weather has resulted in some productive
thinking, however. I have now analysed the behaviour pattern
of the self-steering gear. It seems that speed alone is not the
contributing factor to the breakages, any more than rough
weather or any particular point of sailing. What causes it to
break are the three factors combined in a single moment. Now
if I could steer the boat myself when such conditions were
likely to arise then maybe I could prevent these breakages.
But it's obviously impossible to steer all the time.

I was already steering all day in these conditions and letting
the Sailomat take over at night and trusting to luck. In any event,
I was reasonably confident of reaching Tasmania before all the
spare parts were exhausted.

On 20 December, Day 103, the weather became worse. The
wind, a high-pitched howl in the rigging, penetrated the chart
room and saloon despite my efforts to drown it with the tape-
recorder. I reduced to a storm jib which I again sheeted flat
along the centre line. This kept the speed down so that the
Sailomat could hold the course with the wind on the quarter.
I stayed in my oilskins all night, lying on my bunk ready to
leap on deck the moment anything happened.

Something did happen – at twelve o'clock next day – and it
was dramatic. I suffered a knockdown. I was going on deck and
had just opened the hatch doors when, with an incredible roar,
a wave broke into the cockpit. The force of the water slammed
the doors shut in my face and I could feel the pressure on the
doors from the inside. Some of the water forced its way through
the sides and tops of the doors, and poured into the chart room.
I hung on to the handle and suddenly realized that the boat was

lying over on her side. Seconds went by and I thought 'Come on, *Crusader*, get up', and a few moments later she rolled upright. I pushed the door open and saw the cockpit full to the coaming and the life raft, though held by its fastenings, was floating. Water was rushing everywhere and after the initial confusion I said out loud, 'Get her back on course'. But before I could reach the wheel, yet another wave boiled up from behind. Instead of breaking over the stern it picked *Crusader* up and bore her along at a terrific speed. I thought, 'She's surfing. She's out of control,' but before I could move, the wave subsided and *Crusader* stopped short in a mass of foam and bubbles. I got to the wheel and brought her stern around square to the waves.

I knew the boat must be filling with water but saw with amazement that the self-steering was still working, so I jumped below and lifted the floorboards. There was a lot of water, but it had not yet reached the level of the engine so I pumped frantically till the bilges were nearly empty. Then I jumped on deck again to see if there was any damage. The petrol container roped to the transom had come loose and spilled petrol over everything, so I threw it over the side. Several of the teak gratings were broken and others had disappeared and the contents of the port lockers were strewn around the cockpit. The sails had been tied against the guard rail but fortunately only the corner of the yankee was in the water. I secured it and went to look at the self-steering. The rudder was still attached, but it wasn't working properly because a large piece had broken off the side of the blade. I removed both oar and rudder and started to steer but had to go below every few minutes to check the bilges which were slowly filling again. During these intervals *Crusader*, it seemed, was able to steer herself, so I kept an eye on the course and stayed below to tidy the mess.

After a while the barometer started to rise, but too quickly and the wind increased further. The whole boat shuddered with the force of the storm jib vibrating against the mast and the thud of waves on the hull. I had a schedule with Cape Town Radio and amid shrieking wind and crashing waves I started calling them. To my astonishment I quickly got on to

Rob, but he had such a heavy cold I could hardly understand a word he said. I briefly told him about the knockdown but added that everything was under control. He was his usual encouraging self, although he sounded a little concerned this time. Then the interference became too bad and I had to break off the call.

Following the radio call I crept into my bunk feeling cold, frightened and miserable. After a while I sensed a lull in the wind so I climbed out on deck and started to fit a new rudder on the self-steering. The rudder had suffered such a terrific blow in the knockdown that it was badly bent, and it took me almost three hours of hammering to free it from the shaft. It was nearly dark by the time I had replaced it, but the equipment still wasn't functioning properly. I opened the gear box to see what was wrong and found a control lever had come out of position. I tried to replace it but the movement was so extreme, my arms were so tired and the discomfort of lying stretched out on my stomach so fatiguing that I lost two screwdrivers and a torch overboard and finally had to give up. I went to bed leaving *Crusader* to steer her own rather erratic course through the night.

The next morning started well but ended ominously. Now that I could see properly I repaired the gear box fault in a couple of minutes, but hoisting the No. 2 yankee took me ages as I felt absolutely devoid of energy – due to lack of food, I suspected. If it was, then it led me to do a careless thing which could have been the end of everything. While tightening the wind vane at the top of the self-steering I leaned against the rail to steady myself. I knew this rail was not very secure, but I wasn't unduly perturbed as I was wearing my safety harness. Suddenly the rail came undone, and I fell forwards. I threw my arms around the mast of the wind vane and fortunately, because I had previously tightened it, the mast held and prevented me from falling into the sea. I was shaken but not unduly so. After all, I thought, it couldn't have been too serious because I was wearing my harness. Then I looked around and my blood turned cold; I had forgotten to secure my lifeline to the boat. I now felt so shaky that before attempting to do anything more I went below and cooked myself a six-egg omelette.

The next blight on the day was losing the staysail halyard. I was hoisting the sail when the shackle came undone and the halyard shot up to the top of the mast. There was no way to retrieve it, short of climbing.

By now it was 22 December and I was beginning to feel 'Christmassy'. I needed that halyard but for the moment not vitally; I decided it could wait until after my pre-Christmas wash, thinking that this was the best way to get myself into a Christmas mood. I was standing shivering by the galley with nothing on, when the wind suddenly increased. Wouldn't that just be my luck, I thought: 'Naomi James, round-the-world yachtswoman, found frozen stiff on deck, apparently sunbathing in the Southern Ocean. Yacht miraculously makes its way back to Dartmouth' .... Actually, it would have been difficult to get over the equator and stay frozen, I thought, as I struggled back into my polar suit and went to change to a smaller jib.

The 23rd was another wild night, but I didn't mind because the next day I should be able to turn over the chart, and on the other fold lay Australia! Or a bit of it, anyway. Although it was rough, progress was good and by now I was 2500 miles from Tasmania. In the last four weeks I had covered that number of miles from Cape Town, so was now about halfway. On the afternoon of the 23rd I opened a bottle of red wine, started a new book and wondered what might be in the big box Maureen had put on board labelled 'Happy Christmas'.

I put a note in my log that evening:

I find I want to nibble at things all day. I'm fed up with chocolates and sweets so have taken to chewing crackers. They make a frightful mess everywhere and my sleeping bag is full of crumbs. My cracker-eating bouts have always annoyed Rob who wouldn't eat a dry cracker to save himself. At least I won't get fat.

On Christmas Eve the weather was fairly kind and offered an opportunity to chase the errant halyard. I donned a safety harness and started to climb the mast. The boat was rolling so heavily that I nearly gave up before I reached the spreaders. Then I glanced upwards and it didn't *look* very far, so I continued, but holding on more tightly. Three-quarters of the way up, I had to force myself to keep going; I imagined Rob and Chay watching from the foredeck urging me on (a mixture of scorn and encouragement). I heard Chay say to Rob, 'If she makes it she'll get back to England.' Each separate step required all my strength and for minutes on end I clung to the mast swinging wildly back and forth while I summoned enough will for another step. I was seasick when I got to the top. I reached the block, grabbed the end of the halyard, and started down again, clipping on to each step with my harness. On deck again I crawled back to the cockpit and lay down on the liferaft for a while to recover. It had taken me just over an hour to get up and down the mast. At a later inspection I saw that I had seven new blisters on my hands, and bruises on my arms and legs. None the less it had been a personal triumph, and I was amazed at myself for doing it. Although I didn't take time out to look around while I was up there I had an image of *Crusader*'s deck rolling through areas of white foam amidst large patches of beautiful green, the sort of colour you see off a deep rocky coastline in summer.

I had a short sleep to regain my equilibrium and then thought again about sprucing up for Christmas. I started by giving the saloon a brush-up and polish. I had the radio playing loudly all the time, partly to drown the outside noise and partly to get a good dose of Christmas spirit from the songs and Christmas carols. Radio Australia gave the best reception now although I could still pick up the BBC at times and wanted to listen to it on Christmas Day as Rob was having a request played for me.

Despite all this I was ill at ease as my next log extract shows:

I am reading Irving Stone's *Greek Treasurer*, and it's either that or the reminder of Christmas with all its family connections that has made me feel both emotional and morbid. No matter how much I try to think of the good things and what I shall do when I get home, these thoughts are overshadowed by the fear that I might find death instead. I tell myself that if I'm very careful and if I have a good share of luck there's no real reason to suppose I'll end up in a watery grave. To get home safely to Rob seemed too much to hope for and the completion of this journey too much to achieve. Why couldn't I have been satisfied as navigator of *Great Britain II* and be with him now? The measure of every gain seems to me to relate directly to the depth of misery involved in reaching it. Am I deluding myself by making myself as miserable as possible to buy a safe passage?

The fact that I'm already one-third of the way round the world should be some indication that the next two-thirds can somehow be managed. The potential dangers are: 1) falling overboard; 2) wrecking the boat on some shore through bad navigation; 3) being wrecked in a storm; 4) hitting something – whale, boat, log; 5) going mad, which I think is the most unlikely. I have some control over all of these things, so success or failure really depends on the question of weather conditions. If I have enough sense and seamanship, well, I can only try.

Pre-Christmas blues! Fortunately, it was only Christmas Eve so there was time to have a mope before preparing for the festivities of the next day. That night I had a good sleep, the wind steadied and by morning I was feeling quite cheerful.

My log in the morning:

Christmas Day. First, I opened Maureen's parcel and found a scrumptious feast. Venison soup in wine sauce to start. A whole chicken in brine, which I shall roast with artichokes and asparagus tips, and to follow that – mangoes! Also a bottle of German white wine which is now cooling in the ice bucket (the Southern Ocean). There was a book, too, with a message inside from Maureen and Chay. I shall send them a telegram today.

I went without dinner last night to be sure I had room for this great feast, and this morning I had only a bowl of cereal.

At mid-day I called Rob and spoke to him for the last time before he left on the next leg of the race to Rio which was due to start the following day. I wouldn't, of course, be able to speak to him again until he arrived there, probably in another six weeks. I didn't really mind saying good-bye this time because it reminded me that another stage of the way was over and I was getting nearer home.

My world had shrunk into a blanket of fog and, although it wasn't terribly cold, I nevertheless switched on my cabin heater (a gas heater which worked without a flame) to make the place more cheerful; I also lit two candles. While my dinner was roasting I opened Juliet's present which turned out to be another book and a lollipop. I also looked at the fabulous book about antiques given to me by Rob. He had left it in Cape Town with strict instructions for me not to open the package before Christmas. I hadn't been able to resist opening it to see what he had written, but I only had a *very* quick peep and then put it away for Christmas. I love antiques of any sort and enjoyed the thought, as I looked enviously at the book, that Rob didn't know what he was letting himself in for!

At 9 p.m. I wrote:

I have eaten so much that I have had to sit down for an hour. I opened the wine at three o'clock and now the bottle is nearly empty; oddly enough I am stone-cold sober. I almost had to reef down just before dinner but then the wind suddenly dropped. I was glad; I didn't want to spoil my Christmas by doing another sail change – I have already done two today as it is. I felt a bit weepy when I heard Rob's request on the BBC overseas service, and I have drunk a toast to Rob, the family, Chay and Maureen and friends. Now I am going to bed.

I felt a bit thick-headed when I woke on Boxing Day, but otherwise cheerful and industrious. I washed my hair and used a little fresh water to rinse it in afterwards. Oh, the luxury of clean, silky hair! It felt so nice that I kept looking at myself in my hand mirror, which was all of two inches square. I couldn't see much of my face, but this was just as well, as close scrutiny would certainly have uncovered odd smudges of oil, grease, ink and other marks from jobs I had been doing in the previous few weeks. Then suddenly I remembered that I would be seeing people in less than a fortnight. I had better make myself look a bit more presentable.

My log records the preparations:

> I started with an array of lotion, oils and creams and at the finish felt reincarnated. Not that my face (or what I could see of it) looks much better, but at least it feels good. It hasn't *all* been neglect – it's not that I don't wash, because I do, occasionally. But I never watch what I'm washing as there's a conspicuous absence of full-length mirrors in this place. I defy anyone to stand on a cold wet floor and scrub themselves down with cold, slimy, salt water which refuses to sud, and come up spotless! I can't even get into the bathroom because it's filled with bilge pumps and packets of things, and anyway there's no bath in there. And I'm not allowing myself to use fresh water for washing anyway, let alone gas to heat it with.

I was sitting down on my bunk after lunch a few days later when there was a resounding crash against the hull as though *Crusader* had run into a brick wall. I leapt up on deck and looked down the side expecting to see a gaping hole, but curiously there was nothing, no damage, not even a scratch. At first I thought it must have been a whale or a heavy lump of wood, but then decided it couldn't have been because there were no traces of either; I finally concluded that it must have been a wave. Noticing the course was erratic, I peered over the stern and found the Sailomat rudder had disappeared and only the rope lanyard remained. A chill ran up my spine. I now had only one spare left.

The wind had been moderate to light for nearly a week and the old year seemed to be going out rather meekly, until the very last day when the weather once again began to deteriorate. I wanted to be in festive mood but with a gale in the offing that was difficult. I drank a glass of South African wine, but it had no effect so I returned the bottle to its box and decided instead to make myself some bread. I had some ready-made dough, but either I added too much water, or not enough, or didn't cook it sufficiently. At any rate the result had little in common with normal bread, though I ate it just the same. A little while later I had a stomach-ache.

New Year came and went unnoticed in the established routine of coping with a rolling rocking home with all the associated noises and discomfort. Fortunately, the wind was steady on the bow and I could do without the self-steering gear. It also meant fast sailing, and I made some good days' runs. On the Australia side of my ocean chart I saw that I was on the same line as Perth. Apart from the rendezvous I hardly ever thought of my position in relation to the land; it didn't seem very relevant. Where I travelled it was all sea and only sea and time was in suspension. I might have been away for a week or I might have been away three months. There was nothing to show for my progress except a few lines on a chart.

Cape Town Radio was out of range now and it was Radio Wellington which would be listening out for me in future. I heard them calling and, although my replies were only just audible, at least I had the satisfaction of knowing that my parents would be in contact with the station and would learn that I was still in the land of the living.

On 4 January, Day 118, I saw an incredible sight that made me wonder if someone had dropped an atomic bomb. The whole sky was a mass of light moving in waves and spirals, flickering and glowing as though the world below the horizon was on fire. After gazing at this spectacle in perplexity for a little while it slowly dawned on me what I was witnessing. At the beginning of the trip I'd read Scott's *Voyage to Antarctica*, and he had described this phenomenon as the *Aurora Australis*. I fished out his book and discovered it was something to do with the South Magnetic Pole, but I didn't exactly understand what. I was content to know that it wasn't the world disintegrating. A little while later while taking a last peep I was surprised by *another* light on the horizon. A ship – coming from Antarctica! ! I looked again and blinked. Now there was a whole fleet of them! They were fishing boats. It hadn't occurred to me that there were fishing boats in the Antarctic.

At mid-day on 11 January I wrote:

A predicament. There is a thirty-four-minute difference between the readings of my two sextants. Which one shall I believe? I haven't used the new plastic one before but the mirrors of my Sestral are so tarnished that now I'll have to revert to it. I'll have to look in my books to see how one is supposed to check sextants and discover which of them has the error. I suspect the Sestral.

Next day I made radio contact with New Zealand. Radio Wellington was able to pick up my ETA and my message asking about the spare parts that Sailomat were sending to Tasmania for me; I was to rendezvous there in three days' time. Shortly afterwards, via Radio Melbourne, I was able to speak to the *Hobart Mercury* (the local newspaper which had kindly agreed to arrange things), and I enquired if the spares had arrived. They had terrible news for me. They told me the spares were lost and couldn't be traced. They had apparently left Sweden for Tasmania but none of the airlines had a record of their arrival. Enquiries had been made at all the scheduled calls en route but nothing had come to light. It was now Friday and they should have been at Hobart. The man from the *Mercury* was almost beside himself with worry, and I felt rather sorry for him. I asked if a 24-volt power drill could be sent out with the rendezvous boat instead so that I could try to repair the gear myself.

On the 14th at 4 p.m. I made a perfect landfall. I was delighted but surprised since I had been using the plastic sextant and later discovered that this was the one with the thirty-four-minute error.

I was told the name of the rendezvous boat and its skipper, Bern Cuthbertson, so I called him on the radio and gave my ETA, which was first light the following day. That night the wind blew force seven from the direction of Maatsuyker Island, the place to which I was heading, and by midnight it was obvious that I wouldn't be able to make the rendezvous as planned. I called Bern again and explained the situation and then heard some super news. He told me that the spares had been found and they were on board his boat. Moreover, he said that instead of sailing on to the planned rendezvous point, I should make for the lee of the island and he would meet me there instead.

It was a terribly rough sail, and when I finally came under the sheltered lee of the island I took the sails down and drifted. I was dying for some sleep as I'd had virtually none for two days, so I checked my position carefully with the land and then went to bed.

I was just dropping off when I heard a shout and I thought I must be dreaming. But no, there *was* a shout and it was followed by another . . . and then another. I rushed on deck in panic thinking it was a warning that I was about to go on the rocks, when I saw the shouts were from a fishing boat which had come alongside. I was met with a chorus of greetings. One of the crew held up a crayfish which he was obviously offering to throw aboard. 'I'm afraid I don't like crayfish,' I told him apologetically. I hoped they didn't think me ungrateful.

12
STORMS AND RIGGING DAMAGE

The fishermen were kindness itself; they had heard me talking to the rendezvous boat on the radio and had come over to see if there was anything I needed. They gave me a chart of the southern coast of Tasmania which proved to be invaluable, plus some fish which I *did* like, and then they went on their way. Whilst I was waiting I listened to the weather forecast and learned that a cold front had passed over the area and another was expected within twelve hours. The barometer had been falling throughout the day and was now at an all-time low of 987 millibars. I was anxious to get under way as soon as possible.

Just then I saw a boat approaching so I waited for it to come near. A loud hailer bellowed 'Hello!' It was Bern Cuthbertson. The noise of the wind made speech impossible, so he beckoned me to follow and then led me to the shelter of a small island. On arrival he handed me the self-steering spares, fresh fruit, including cherries and grapes, some butter, bread, milk and my mail! It was like Christmas all over again. But I couldn't delay because the weather looked threatening and I had to make repairs to the storm jib as well as assemble the Sailomat rudder. The new rudder was fantastic, very solid and strong, and they had obviously re-designed it. It certainly looked as though I wouldn't have to worry about the self-steering gear again.

As I left the rendezvous the wind was coming in savage bursts and I could only set the storm jib which unfortunately kept the speed down. I knew that I had to clear the eastern tip of

Tasmania, Cape Pillar, forty-five miles distant, before I would be back in clear water again.

All went well for the rest of the day, although I was very uneasy about the look of the sky. Streaks and spirals, dense grey in colour, stretched from horizon to horizon. I'd never seen anything like it before. The barometer had settled ominously on 987 millibars.

I couldn't risk sleeping until I had passed a group of unlit rocks offshore. I thought it was very unfair of nature to scatter silly little rocks in awkward places like that. I didn't see them but I estimated I'd passed them by dark and as I was by then dog-tired, I disconnected the Sailomat and ran down wind with just the storm jib sheeted in tight, hoping to get a little sleep. It was unusually squally and I didn't want to risk my precious new rudder so soon.

At midnight I was back in my oilskins, peering anxiously into the gloom where the land lay. By 2 a.m. *Crusader* was starting to surf and broach. I put my harness on and I had a last glance at the barometer. An hour earlier it had dropped another 2 millibars, but now it was shooting up again. I pumped the bilges, secured the hatch doors and went to the helm. All hell was breaking loose. The noise was deafening. The wind was coming in wild blasts every few seconds, and the air was filled with flying spray which by the light of the torch looked like rain. The compass bulb had blown and I had to hold the torch in my teeth to see the course I was steering. I couldn't look backwards or sideways because of the spray and rain.

After an hour I was freezing and shaking with fear. The mast looked as if it might come down any minute, and the top hank of the jib had ripped free. This caused the halyard to come slack and vibrate, and I had to crawl along the deck to try and tighten it. The wind tore into me as soon as I stood by the mast and heaved down on the winch handle. On the foredeck I could feel the rigging shuddering under the blows. *Crusader* was going much too fast and I was thinking desperately about how to get her under control. The technique of streaming rope warps over the stern came to mind. Because of *Crusader*'s size I didn't think it would work but, despite my reservations, I thought I had better try. First, I took the two jib sheets, tied them together with bowlines and threw the loop over the stern. It didn't seem to make any difference, so I tied two more jib sheets and a long orange warp which was very light but quite thick. It was frayed in places so I tied knots here and there and paid it out as well. The effect was immediate. Every time she began to surf the warps would drag along the surface sending up clouds of spray and seemed almost to stop the boat in her tracks. She was now sailing down wind without my help, and the speed was reduced to four or five knots.

Now that she was under control I went below to try and work out my position – half my fear was not knowing exactly where I was. The wind had backed to the SW and I was afraid this might put me on to Cape Pillar. My dead reckoning put me ten to fifteen miles off the Cape, and if the wind didn't back any further, I would clear it, but only with a few miles to spare. It was very frightening.

While I had been on deck the barometer had risen to 1002 – a massive jump which accounted for the incredible wind strength. It was now getting light, so I went up on deck again to have a look around, and there, to my immeasurable relief, was the headland. The description in the Pilot book confirmed that the basalt cliffs and strange-shaped islands around about were indeed Cape Pillar. It was already about fifteen miles away, so unless the wind went round to the south I would pass at a safe distance. I felt much better.

When the sun came out the scene was quite spectacular. Black squalls raced low overhead and brilliant white combers tumbled all around me. Despite the spray and periodic squalls the visibility was marvellous. The faraway rocks gleamed in the early light, and I felt fortunate that because the wind had stayed where it was they remained a distant vision.

At 10 a.m. the wind lulled and at 3 p.m. I was totally and infuriatingly becalmed. I could still see the coast but ignored it and thought about my next landfall, the Foveaux Strait, between Stewart Island and the South Island of New Zealand. It was less than 900 miles away and that meant about eight days' sailing.

The cold front was followed closely by a gigantic high which stayed with me for three weeks, giving very light winds for the first three days, then steady northerlies. It was warm with lovely starry nights, and for a little while I was able to forget about gales and concentrate on more pleasant subjects.

My radio contact improved and on the third day after leaving Tasmania I spoke to my parents, Fiona, Brendan and virtually everyone else in the family. They were waiting for my call because I had sent them a telegram with the time I would be ringing. There was so much laughter and background chatter during the call that it made me feel I was back home in the living room. Mother had obviously been practising her radio technique because she came through clear and precise – except for the occasional unprofessional hoot of laughter. My father confided he was unhappy to talk on the phone because he was going deaf and might miss something important! Brendan and I had a perfectly unintelligible conversation about whales, waffling on and on, and we would have continued for ever if we hadn't been interrupted by Fiona who wanted to know where and when I would be sailing past New Zealand. I told her I should be off the South Island on 24 January. Unfortunately our home was on the North Island, so they wouldn't be able to wave to me as I sailed by.

I enjoyed myself in the warm and calm weather and could now spend much more time on deck which made such a change from the past two months. I spent a little time doing some repairs to the sails and invariably had my radio tuned to the World Service of Radio Australia. It was the clearest English-speaking station in those latitudes, and once I had become used to the accents I found the programmes very amusing.

During the next radio call to the family I heard the latest race report. All the yachts were round the Horn and Rob was in the lead! ! *Great Britain II* always went well in bad weather, and I wondered if that was what the conditions had been like. Also,

Mother gave me the recipe for her scones which I asked for, and my father told me he was worried about the lack of rain and low wool prices.

The closer I sailed to New Zealand the more alarmed I became at the thought of having to go through a narrow gap which, from the chart, looked like the eye of a needle. Two hundred miles from Stewart Island I made my decision.

I wrote in my log:

After close scrutiny and careful consideration of the Pilot book, I have decided not to go through the Foveaux Strait after all. The reason – I am a coward. It just looks too formidable, and I see no reason to tackle it when I don't have to – I can just as easily steer to the south of Stewart Island. Since the episode off Cape Pillar in Tasmania I want to avoid land and lee shores as much as possible. Navigationally speaking the only disadvantage in this new course is that it will take me further to the south and I shall have to watch out for some unlighted rocks off shore. The other and biggest disadvantage is that I won't be able to hand anyone the twelve-page letter I've written to Rob. If he has to wait till the Azores it will have grown into a manuscript!

24 January (Day 138)
I feel better now that I have decided to steer south. The thought of the Strait must have been bothering me; something certainly has been on my mind because I have felt oddly unsettled since leaving Tasmania. This little hop across the Tasman Sea is only a warm-up before getting into stride for the big stuff. New Zealand is just an annoying hazard. (This is not the way I usually think of my country!) It's unsettling also to be so close to a former way of life and yet now to be so separate from it. Hearing the familiar voices of family secure in their usual occupations gives me a feeling of unreality. It is as though I am not really here at all. I've been reading the New Zealand Pilot book avidly to remind myself of the terrain, flora and geography of New Zealand, and the outlying uninhabited islands look very desirable. Some of them are only inhabited by mutton birds and have no vegetation or water. What do the birds drink? Sea water?

If anchoring wasn't such a mammoth task for a single-hander on a yacht of this size, then I should be tempted to visit one of the islands and pay my respects to the mutton birds.

I passed to the south of Stewart Island in the fog on the night of the 24th. It was a sleepless night because I had to go between two small groups of islands called the Snares and the Traps which, of course, remained invisible to me. At 9 a.m. next morning I saw the coast of Stewart Island low on the horizon. That would be my last glimpse of land until I reached South America.

I now discovered with delight that I had sufficient batteries to play my big transistor without worrying. When a song came on which I liked, I would turn up the volume and either make a precarious attempt to dance, or I would sing at the top of my voice. Occasional birds cruising past would look askance, but on the whole they didn't object to the sound or the spectacle. It struck me as odd that the birds held so little curiosity for me, as if there were yachts in their waters every day of the week.

On 1 February, I was back in the old rough-weather routine. The previous week's run had been a record for me – just under 1000 miles in seven days, at an average of 140 miles a day. Even this didn't match up with Chichester's good runs, and moreover his course was very much further north where the winds were reputedly lighter and less consistent.

However, racing against Chichester's time gave me an incentive. His boat had been faster than mine, but against that he had stopped in Sydney for several weeks so our overall times were now about equal. I still had a chance to beat him. I worked it out that I should have to be back in England by 10 June, and if I could reach the Horn by 14 March, I had a good chance.

That evening I wrote in my log:

After five months I still find it difficult to explain – even to myself – why I am making this trip. The fact that the opportunity to do so presented itself was obviously not the

sole reason; there was a deeper motivation than that. Do I
want fame and recognition? I don't think so, and, anyway,
while that motive could have been strong enough to make me
set out, alone it certainly wouldn't have been strong enough to
sustain me this far.

I have always been slightly afraid of other people,
imagining that they are looking down at my faults and finding
obvious inadequacies. I feel that I am out here to escape from
this criticism, or perhaps it is the subconscious desire to prove
to myself, and to the world, that such criticism is unjust. Yes,
that must be it – to prove that I am a rational, self-dependent
and capable human being, one who has consciously chosen to
try and live at the upper levels of man's capabilities and at
the same time survive. I think I also enjoy showing that it is
not necessary to accept, as most people do, the way of life that
is expected of them on account of their background and
education. If you want to do something different you can.

The beauty about my life at sea alone is that my limits are
the extent of my physical and psychological make-up. I
succeed or fail by my own endeavours without any influence
from the outside world. I like being a free agent and an
individual which is perhaps why I am against all religion and
political doctrines which try and impose their will on
mankind.

It must have been the effect of the bad weather again which
made me indulge in such introspection.

A few days later I was again thinking of home and Rob. I sat
at the chart table in the dark after dinner with a cassette of our
favourite songs and thought of our old MGB racing along with
the hood down in the hills above Kingswear. Although we had
only lived in South Devon two years, and then more absent
than not, I had thought of it as home. I loved the sleepy streets
and the wooded path above Waterhead Creek where Rob and I
used to walk with his parents and their Alsatians. We had a
super little cottage, but even so I had set my heart on living in a
secluded farmhouse up in the hills. With a few acres of land and
some animals we could live out the rest of our lives in utter
contentment. But now I began to realize that it was unimportant

which country we settled in, as long as Rob was there. I should surround myself with all my books and lovely pieces of antique furniture, and wherever we were it would be an earthly heaven.

When I was feeling low I'd sometimes get out the photo album, which went back to the time we first met, and slowly thumb through the pages. It reminded me that there was another world besides this present one which was quite real even though it had faded into obscurity. In the album there were pictures of Rob and Chay on *Great Britain II*, which prompted me to get out my pen and write:

> Rob taught me to sail and navigate just over two years ago and by now must have faith in my ability. And so must Chay. But do they *really* know? I wonder how they can possibly know what I am capable of. This business doesn't only depend on skill, and besides, they know I'm not *that* skilful. So what makes them think that I can sail a boat round the world alone? Is it because I say I can do it? Yes, I think that is the answer. *They* believe I can do it because *I* believe I can, and such a belief in a person's determination is an incredible expression of faith. But if I *fail*, then, in the eyes of the world, they will be the ones to blame. And they won't be able to exonerate themselves by saying she died because she made a mistake, even if it were the truth.
>
> Poor Rob. I'll have to make it. It would be just too terrible if I didn't.

To avoid becoming too gloomy I didn't often allow such thoughts to develop, but it was remarkable how they suddenly entered my mind for no apparent reason. Thoughts that had been puzzling me for years, suddenly clarified themselves and I found I could now make sense of them. Once, back in the Vienna days, I had written down everything that I felt deeply about, but mostly in the form of questions. Now, although I didn't have all the answers, I found the practice of writing had helped to straighten things out in my mind. Now, in fact, I was learning to do my thinking without the aid of a diary.

I did, however, write my journal every day because I thought it would be worthwhile to have an accurate record and, of course, it would be useful if I ever came to write a book about my voyage later. But I never wrote at length on any philosophical subject unless it was relevant to the business of the day.

On 3 January I spoke to Pop and Brendan, both of whom were very cheery, having just come back from the pub. Brendan wanted to know why I hadn't recently sent a telegram to the pub to help them keep their chart up to date! I hadn't appreciated the tremendous interest shown by the locals in my progress. They remembered me from my shearing days, and would come into the pub and study the chart avidly.

Mother's scone recipe had been a disaster in my hands so next time I hopefully added garlic and jam to the ingredients. The result was indescribably awful. The truth was that my diet was beginning to pall. The loaf of fresh bread and butter that I'd been given at the rendezvous had reminded my stomach that there were other things besides tinned and dehydrated foods, and what I was now experiencing was a kind of rebellion. I had a sack of All Bran and thought about making another batch of scones. But the smell of the bran reminded me of biscuits rather than scones for some obscure reason, so I set about turning the All Bran into biscuits. I had never made biscuits before, but I thought it couldn't be difficult. I melted some margarine, added some sugar, four handfuls of bran, two eggs and two spoons of cocoa and flour, stirred the mixture until it was smooth. I then cut little squares and put them in the oven. And what do you know . . . ! They turned out surprisingly like real bran cakes. For dinner that evening I tried out a new concoction of tuna fish in white sauce with onions and peas. That was good, too.

Fortunately hunger was a good incentive to cook, otherwise I wouldn't have bothered. My will-power was surprisingly weak when it came to doing routine, perfectly easy things like cleaning my teeth or putting on my oilskins to go on deck.

I also noticed I was becoming increasingly absent-minded. For instance, I'd start working out a sight, and halfway through I would decide that the bilges needed pumping; that would make me thirsty so I would then put on the kettle and have a cup of tea, and then my eyes would light on a book so I'd begin to read. Sometime later my thoughts would wander back to the day's run and I'd suddenly remember that I was supposed to be working out a sight!

There were other times, especially when it was rough, when I'd sit for hours at the chart table staring vaguely into space and thinking about nothing in particular. But I was never ever bored, even during these reflective periods, and this was most important. Being on my own encouraged me to fill my time with some sort of satisfactory occupation. My aversion to boredom gave me enough discipline to use my time constructively and not to fall into a state of apathy. It also helped to have so many different interests on board apart from working the boat; if I grew tired of reading I would spend a few days just carving, or writing my journal or letters to Rob.

On 6 February, Day 152, the weather was really miserable. Early in the morning I had been trying to raise someone on the radio, but the wind suddenly rose from nothing to force six, and I had to dash on deck to drop the sails and change down to storm canvas. The wind was from ahead and within a short time I could no longer beat to windward so was forced to run off to the west, streaming warps to keep the speed as low as possible. Running in a gale in the wrong direction was a slow form of torture, and I often wondered what Chay or Chichester would have done. Chay had had to face this sort of thing quite often and even though *British Steel* was designed for windward sailing he almost certainly had to give up and lie-a-hull sometimes. I would have liked to have risked it but thought the waves were too big just to lie doggo, and I would have hated the strain of waiting to see if a big one would knock *Crusader* down.

The rain was continuous, and I kept the heater on to absorb the damp. The heater also helped to dry out the wet patches caused by leaks and, most importantly, dry out my polar suit which was stiff with salt. Every few hours I tried to contact Radio Wellington, as I was already overdue. I thought of poor Rob, yet again in port with no word from me, but the line was silent each time except for a few crackles and noises like a squirrel spitting out peanut husks.

On the 8th I noted in my log:

I'm entering a familiar mid-ocean limbo which will last until I get to the second half of the eastern sheet. (I've still got a thin slice of New Zealand on this half.) It is amazing to have a large chart showing nothing but sea and the odd reef, but I now know that I'm not afraid of the sea. I hate stormy weather, but I can't regard the sea as evil or unfriendly; after all it's just the same water that one finds in a bath tub – more or less. The birds certainly don't seem to mind it. No matter what the state of the sea the enormous white albatrosses sweep across its surface, gently fingering the wave tops with their wings, silent, ghostlike and entirely at home in their bleak environment. At least they appear big enough to stand the bad weather, but what about the tiny Mother Cary's chickens? They would look decidedly more at home splashing in a bird bath than tripping daintily down the sides of mountainous waves. I was watching a bird this afternoon – I think it was a Molly hawk – circling round and round, never once flapping its wings, and I wondered how the devil he did it.

10 February (Day 156) an unexpected diversion:

Oh, what a lovely morning! I've been running in the rain, collecting raindrops and getting wet. I wore my polar suit to wash out the salt and rigged up a big plastic bag as a water-collecting device under the mainsail. In it I collected enough in drips to fill a five-gallon container, and I washed myself from head to toe in lovely soft soapy water. Now I'm squeaky clean. The rain has brought a rise in temperature, which even made washing a pleasure. The chart room looks as if it has been hit by a waterfall, but the heater will dry it out.

After a few days the weather changed and calm prevailed again. I wrote:

Damn these perverse and cursed calms!! They make my blood boil. It was blowing well yesterday and to make the maximum number of miles I steered for a whole twelve hours. Now the wind has disappeared and I'm left with the usual offering of glassy swells which come and go from all directions. I should really take the sails down and wait for some wind, but *Crusader* has managed to make the odd knot which is at least a slight improvement on staying in one place. The only way to beat this weather is to try and keep busy and ignore it. I've cleaned and greased all the tools which I noticed were starting to rust. I've also cut out one pink and one mauve elephant from some decorative wrapping paper and stuck them over those instrument dials which are no longer working. The wrapping paper came from Juliet's parcel – should have been white elephants. Parts of the boat's interior are getting badly stained with mould and water marks and the small cabin where the spares and tools are kept is particularly affected; but I can't do much about the situation, as fresh water is too precious, and scrubbing the mouldy areas with salt water will only make things worse. I'll tackle the whole boat once I get back to the Doldrums.

The egg locker was beginning to smell too much for me to overlook, so I searched inside and fished out the offenders and the smell subsided. I was beginning to think all the eggs might be going off, but the remaining three dozen seemed fine. They tasted vaguely of mould, but that was something I was prepared to accept.

By now I was getting short of provisions – at least those that I liked most, such as tinned mince and onions, French long-life bread, potato salad and grapefruit juice. I only had six reasonable onions left, which for me was a real tragedy. I liked onions with most things I cooked, since they disguised the taste of canned foods. But the most precious vegetables on board at that moment were the two remaining pumpkins. They were dry and wrinkled-looking but still fresh. I was loth to eat these last two, but I decided to finish them on the next special occasion and make a real feast.

On 19 February, Day 165, I got a message from my parents that Rob would be expecting me to call the next morning at 3 a.m. – Rio time! I thought it was an extraordinary time to be calling him, but I made the schedule with Radio Wellington. However, I was doubtful that he would be there to receive my call because I was under the impression that the number I had been given was not a private home or hotel but a yacht club. To my vast surprise when I called at the arranged time he answered straight away. Unfortunately, the line was bad and we could hardly hear each other, so we agreed to try again twenty-four hours later. But nevertheless I was frustrated at not being able to say more than a simple hello and good-bye, and for the rest of the day remained restless and worried in case something prevented me from speaking to him the next day.

On the 20th I tried once more and after further frustrations and hold-ups Rob finally came through. This time the line was much better. He answered all the questions that I had prepared, and most important of all he was able to tell me the position of the Antarctic ice limit for February. He himself had had bad weather, but not as much as he had experienced in the same race four years earlier. The final leg of the race to Portsmouth was due to begin in a few hours, so it was good-bye again until April when he reached England. He asked if I had any problems, and I said no. 'Well, keep your chin up,' he said. 'Push on and you'll be home before you know it!'

As it transpired I was able to speak to Rob again five weeks later, but even if I had known that at the time it still wouldn't have tempered the sadness I felt as I put the hand set down. It was a long time to wait in any case, but specially as I was embarking on the most crucial stage of the trip. However, in all other respects I was in good spirits. I had 2500 miles to go before I reached Cape Horn and a further 1000 miles before I entered the more familiar and friendly Atlantic. The weather had been bad, but I didn't think it would get any worse, and I now felt that *Crusader* could handle any sort of weather conditions. All the equipment on board was in good shape and my self-steering problems were greatly minimized. I was feeling fit and ready to take on the last part of the Southern Ocean.

Three days later, on 23 February, I was much less confident:

The weather has turned nasty. I was hoping for a good sleep
this morning but have been up since five. Even earlier I was
constantly jumping to my feet when unusually heavy squalls
descended. I saw an awesome crimson sunrise which reminded
me of all the evil portents attached to this phenomenon. On
the lighter side it looked like a sky Delacroix might have
painted, except that the charging horses were missing – I
supposed the squalls had got them. At 9 a.m. I lowered the
mainsail; *Crusader* was being tossed about a good deal by the
short steep waves thrown up in front of the squalls. And for
some reason the yankee was vibrating like mad, which got on
my nerves, so I altered course off the wind to ease the situation.
The barometer fell a few points but has now steadied, brewing
up its next wicked move. Ah, well, we battle on. Things
could be worse and I suppose I ought to be getting used to
this sort of thing. . . .

At six o'clock in the morning of the 24th there was a clatter
on deck. Any new or strange noise usually brings bad news, but
this was catastrophic. When I got up on deck I could do nothing
but hold my breath and stare in horror at the mast. It was
bending from side to side with each roll of the boat and on the
deck, collapsed in a heap, were the starboard lower shrouds.

13
CAPSIZE ON THE APPROACH TO CAPE HORN

After a few seconds I ran to the mast and pulled down the mainsail. That left the storm jib set, and I let its halyard go. But then I saw that with no sail to steady it the mast's movement was even more pronounced, so I quickly hoisted the jib again. I stood back and looked. It was the leeward shrouds that were down and not the ones that had the weight – the ones on the windward side. This was strange but fortunate for if the windward ones had collapsed the mast would probably have gone.

After I'd watched for a few moments I decided it didn't look about to topple, so I climbed aloft to check the fittings which held the lower shrouds on the windward side. They seemed secure. I then looked on the other side of the mast to discover what had caused the shrouds to collapse, and saw that the fitting which held them had sheered. I climbed down and looked around for some immediate way to steady the mast, even if only temporarily. I thought the heavy rope spinnaker guys might do the job. They were in the cockpit locker, so I dragged one out and climbed back up the mast to make the end fast beneath the spreaders at the point of the broken fitting. Then I led the free end through a block which I fixed to the deck, and winched tight. I looked aloft and saw with relief that the mast had now stopped swaying. After that I went back to my bunk and assessed the situation. I couldn't sail with the mast in its precarious state, so the first thing was to decide how to strengthen it. Could I get the shrouds back up again?

The fitting which attached the shrouds to the mast consisted of a fork-shaped plate which, in turn, was held with a long stainless-steel bolt through the mast. Each shroud was fixed to the fork ends of the plate, and it was these that had broken. If I could drill a hole in each severed plate then perhaps it would be possible to fit them back by placing them over the bolt. That's if I could undo the nut. . . .

Meanwhile, the overall situation looked fairly serious. I didn't know how long the mast would hold with rope, and I dared not put up more sail till I had repaired it more satisfactorily. I gave a fleeting thought to my position and then immediately put it out of mind – 2800 miles from New Zealand and 2200 from the Horn was not a prospect to contemplate. I stayed in my bunk for a little while to get warm while I decided what part of the planned operation to tackle first.

Breakfast seemed a good idea; going up the mast twice before eating had made my legs wobble like jelly. I heated some spaghetti but had to force it down. Then I hunted amongst the spares for tools and likely looking materials for the repair job.

At 1 p.m. I wrote in my log:

Things look black. I've been up the mast twice and, even though the wind has lulled somewhat, the effort of hanging on is exhausting. First, I tried to loosen the nut on the bolt, but it wouldn't budge – furthermore, it looks very much as if it won't be long enough to carry the two plates I want to put on. However, it's still worth a further try. I do have another bolt which is thinner and longer, and though not ideal it is better than nothing. I drilled a hole in one of the plates and then had to file it to fit the bolt. What a blessing I brought along a kitchen steel.

The barometer is still falling and it's raining. No sign yet of a wind change. Trying to sail with the prospect of a gale in the offing is pointless, but I've left the jib hoisted and I'm jogging along at two to three knots. I've rigged an extra spinnaker guy so now I have two replacement shrouds. I also have my bosun's chair ready which will allow me to sit while I work, and, if I tie it to the mast, this will also mean I have two free hands and don't have to use all my strength to hang on. The awful truth is that there's no chance of a flat sea in

which to do the job; such things don't exist in these parts and
when there's a calm, the rolling becomes worse than ever.
A light wind with the boat close hauled would probably
produce the steadiest motion, but I don't suppose I'll get it.

Now the reaction's setting in and what at first I thought
would be easy I now realize to be very involved. Still, there
has to be a way. If only the weather would be kind to me. . . .

I'm going to try to have a little sleep. I feel so devoid of
strength and I'm sure it's lack of sleep.

At 3 p.m. I wrote:

Couldn't sleep – too apprehensive. I'm going on with the
drilling. I've just realized the barometer and weather are
behaving in the same way that they did when I was off
Tasmania.

As soon as it was dark I crept miserably into my bunk to wait
for the night to pass. The weather was obviously brewing
something horrible, but I tried not to let my mind dwell on the
memories of the storm off Tasmania.

Then the following morning I wrote:

The weather didn't break in the night, but the barometer kept
falling until it had reached 987 millibars. I thought of
another way to fix the shrouds when I couldn't sleep so this
morning I rose early, had tea and toast, and put on my
oilskins. I got the bosun's chair out and put a spare harness
round the mast to stop me from spinning. In addition I had a
crescent spanner, mole grips and a socket spanner with
ratchet – all tied to my harness with bits of string (a
precaution after losing my best spanner yesterday). It was
much easier to work from the chair tied in position, although
I still suffered bruised legs from being flung from side to side.

My new idea was to overlap and bolt the broken pieces on
to the original plate, but it was unworkable because there was
too little material to drill. Still, after two hours of struggling I
managed to free the nut from the bolt which was something I
had been unable to do yesterday.

I was feeling relatively pleased with myself at the finish
until I had a close look at the fitting on the other side of the

mast and saw to my horror that it had also cracked. And it had cracked in exactly the place where the starboard side shroud had parted. As the port shrouds were in danger of coming down as well, I rigged guys on that side, too. There was absolutely nothing further I could do, and with so much else to worry about I simply carried on with the job of drilling.

The night of 25 February I wrote in my log:

Today seems to have lasted for ever. I spent the rest of the morning drilling and filing, then at mid-day, as there was still no wind and the barometer was more or less steady, I decided to go all out and see if I could get the job finished.

I climbed the mast to fit the new bolt and then found that it wasn't even as long as the old one! How could that possibly be? I was so absolutely certain that it was longer. I felt defeated, even cheated and so depressed I could have sat down and cried. I now had to go back to the original bolt hoping that it might just be long enough; it was already too late in the day to file the larger holes in the plates to the size which the thicker bolt required. As a desperate measure I fixed the shrouds with a snap shackle secured to the bolt – even that took me over two hours.

When I finally got back down to the deck the weather was breaking, and within minutes gale force gusts and rain were sweeping across the sea. I tied the sails more securely, removed all loose items on deck and stowed them down below. The barometer had risen several millibars in the last few hours, and I hoped it wouldn't begin to rise too fast. There was a deep blue hue all round the horizon which definitely wasn't blue sky.

It's now 23.00 and I've been trying for the last hour to make contact with Radio Wellington. I can hear them very clearly, but they don't seem to hear me at all. All this after I have made such an effort to hoist the aerial. It meant going up the mast yet again to free it from the temporary shrouds. I wanted to call Rob and let him know what had happened. Now it appears I can't even do that.

The starboard shrouds came down again at seven o'clock next morning. I couldn't see what had broken, and it was too rough to climb the mast. Still, the port shrouds with the cracked fittings were holding and so were my spinnaker guys; I only hoped the nut had stayed on the bolt. The weather was doing its best for me and the wind hadn't increased above force eight. The barometer, too, was rising slowly.

I began to consider the options that the situation presented: if I could make a reasonable repair, then I would press on to the Falkland Islands. If the repair was less satisfactory then I had to think of another plan, because the mast would be unable to stand up to the type of storms possible at the Horn. What about a port in South America? I wondered. I looked at the chart, but there seemed to be no suitable place south of latitude 30°. Besides, I had no large-scale charts with which to navigate along the coast. Then again the boat would probably not be able to sail satisfactorily to windward as often demanded in coastal sailing. I thought about returning to New Zealand, but was very loth to do that, as it would mean delaying my passage round the Horn until the following year. Also I would still have about 3000 miles of windward sailing simply to get there.

I concluded that the most favourable course was to make for the Falkland Islands, but to do so meant that at all costs I had to make a good job of repairing the mast.

In the meantime, the barometer had stopped at 999 mlb and was falling slowly again, and the wind had died away. I had spent the morning drilling holes in the shroud plate to fit the larger bolt, and while I was doing this I hit on an alternative idea. I wasn't certain that these plates would fit over the bolt so I decided to wind a wire strop around the mast and spreaders. At least it would be secure and hold in place even if it did obstruct the sail track and make it impossible to hoist the mainsail to its proper height.

By early afternoon the plates were ready with the holes now large enough to take a reasonable-sized rigging screw. I took the strop up the mast, having previously hoisted the shrouds on a halyard so that they would be in easy reach from my chair. I fixed the strop, secured the shrouds to it, and the arrangement seemed to go together quite well, except that I was disappointed to see it was impossible to tighten them sufficiently. The strop with its plates was obviously too long and would have to be shortened. However, I found myself with no time left to do this by then because the weather had worsened.

Another nagging fear, although it had lately diminished in comparison to my others, was the excessive play in the main rudder. The play appeared to be getting progressively worse and now – on top of it all – I had to consider the possibility that the rudder might fall off. What should I do? Go on . . . or go back? What would Rob have done? If only I could ask him. Even if I could have got a telegram to him, however, it would have taken perhaps a week to get a reply, and I had to make an immediate decision. I was very depressed and I ached badly from all the climbing.

My overall sailing time seemed to be of little consequence now that the fate of the trip itself hung in the balance, but by the evening of 26 February, two days after the rigging failure, I was seriously considering yet another alternative course. With the weather deteriorating rapidly, my fear and apprehension grew – then suddenly I had a brilliant idea. I would give up the plan to sail around the world via the Horn and go through the Panama Canal instead! It would mean returning to New Zealand where the rigging could be repaired, collecting more charts and then going on. It would add many more miles, but it was still worth considering. It was an exciting idea because it represented the possibility of turning defeat into something less than defeat. As I felt at the time I could no longer contemplate carrying on around the Horn and facing further punishment from the Southern Ocean.

26 February (Day 172)
6 p.m.: Goodness how I ache! I can feel every muscle and bruise acutely. Priorities now are: 1) to survive this weather; 2) to rig better shrouds; 3) to head north.

Fierce squalls pass every ten minutes or so, fifty-knotters at least. Each one builds up its own nasty waves and one of them has just broken right over *Crusader*. I saw it coming as I was looking out of the window, and I hung on. Luckily she didn't heel too far over. If only the barometer would rise. I've been lying-a-hull or just creeping forward with the storm jib for almost three days now, and I know that it could last a lot longer. I wish I had a way of cheering myself up. I've started re-reading one of the books in my library but haven't been able to concentrate at all.

Sometimes I lie in my bunk for an hour at a time, and to stop myself from staring at the barometer I gaze through the skylight at the rigging and sky, which doesn't make me feel any better. I can't sleep.

8 p.m. I'm soon going to be faced with the decision as to whether I should stay lying-a-hull and risk capsize, or steer down wind and risk personal injury from waves breaking over the stern. The thought of the way that wave bent the self-steering rudder gives me the shudders. There's a good force eight now with horrible squalls, and every now and again a wave bangs into *Crusader* with a shocking thud. I am running the engine in order to charge the batteries in case Radio Wellington try to contact me tonight. At least the diesel drowns the noise outside, and with the cabin light switched on the world seems quite friendly – so long as I don't look out.

I've made some re-arrangements down below and put the heavy things like boxes of tinned margarine and bags of sugar into empty lockers which can be fastened shut. Until now they have lain secured by lee-cloths on the top bunk: safe now, but hardly so in the event of a capsize.

Just before it got dark, I watched the effect of a squall coming over the sea. The waves were flattened, but the surface boiled under the furious wind. When a squall hits it shakes the mast and yet there isn't a shred of sail up. To drown the noise I am now playing the cassette, in place of the engine, and trying to deaden my mind with a glass of port.

On the 27th, that which I had always dreaded happened. Hours later I wrote in my log:

I capsized at 0.500 this morning. I was only half awake at the time, but suddenly aware that the wind had increased even beyond the prevailing force ten. It was just daylight, and I was trying to make up my mind whether to get up and try steering when I heard the deafening roar of an approaching wave. I felt the shock, a mountain of water crashed against *Crusader*'s hull, and over she went. An avalanche of bits and pieces descended on me as she went under, and I put up my arms to protect my face. After a long and agonizing pause she lurched up again. I don't recall the act of climbing out of my bunk or even my sleeping bag. but I found myself well and truly free of them both.

As far as I remember, my first move was to look through the skylight at the rigging. It scarcely registered that the mast was still standing. I could hear water running into the bilges, so I quickly started to pump. For a terrible moment I felt that she was sinking, but as I pumped I could see the level going down. I pumped in a frenzy for a few minutes and then jumped on deck to see if the mast and rigging were really all right.

I noticed one spinnaker pole had gone and the other was broken. The sails which had been lashed along the guard rails were dragging in the water. I hauled them aboard somehow and re-tied them to the rails. The radio aerial was flying loose, and the deck fitting from which it had been torn was now letting in water. As a temporary measure I plugged it with an old T-shirt and returned below to continue pumping the bilges. There was a strong smell of paraffin and milk. All the stores on the top bunk had been hurled out and the lee-cloth hung in shreds. My main concern was that she might go over again, so I left things below as they were, dug out some thick socks, gloves, hat and oilskins (all wet) and went to the helm to steer.

I secured my safety harness to the compass binnacle and faced the waves so that I could see them coming. The vision scared me stiff. The waves were gigantic, a combination of twenty-foot swells with twenty- to thirty-foot waves on top. One crashed near by, and it didn't need any imagination to realize what would happen if one of these monsters fell on me.

Suddenly *Crusader* started to surf, and I gripped the wheel desperately to keep the stern directly on to the wave and hold her straight. The next wave picked her up like a toy and wrenched all control from me. There was nothing but mountains of water everywhere, like waterfalls. The speed was impossible to gauge as there was nothing to judge it by, and the water all round me was at deck level, seething and hissing as if on the boil. Finally, the wave passed and she slowed down. I started to cry from a feeling of helplessness at being out of control and caught at the mercy of one of those awful waves. But I still had to leave the wheel to pump the bilges. When I got back to the wheel a wave broke over the stern, and I threw my arms round the binnacle as the water cascaded over me and filled the cockpit. Fortunately the volume of water wasn't too alarming. What was the lesser evil, I wondered: capsizing or being crushed by a wave? What would Rob do? Keep on top of the situation and trust to luck. I had to accept the dismal thought that there was only me here with my quota of luck; I steered numbly onwards and hoped that my luck would last.

On the fourth occasion that I went below to pump I saw the barometer was 1003 and rising slowly. I was confronted by a terrible mess, but the biggest things had held in place; there was no actual damage except for odd dents and scars on the roof of the saloon. My neck was very sore – somehow I must have pulled a muscle at the moment of capsize because I was aware of aches as soon as I reached the deck.

I steered on devoid of thought and incapable of feeling. At 10.30 a.m. I detected a lull, followed half an hour later by another. At last I began to feel better, and when on a trip below I saw a bottle of port rolling in a corner and took a swig. I also grabbed some water biscuits and ate them at the wheel.

At 11.30 the wind was down to force eight, but I kept steering until 2 p.m., by which time the wind had reduced to intermittent heavy squalls. It now seemed safe, so I left her lying-a-hull. The radio was drenched but it worked, and after an hour of con-centrated cleaning up the interior was almost back to normal. However, there seemed to be a curious itinerary of missing items, including my fountain pen, the can opener, hairbrush and kettle. Most of my crockery was broken. A bad moment was finding my Salalite transistor quite dead; that meant no more time signals to check the error of my chronometer. Still, the clock was quartz and kept very good time, and there was no reason to think it might suddenly become erratic.

My bed was sopping wet, but fortunately I had a spare sleeping bag stowed away in a plastic bag. I hauled it out in triumph – bone dry! The cabin heater soon dried out my pillow. I had no dry footwear and on the floor was a slippery mixture of milk, paraffin and bilge water.

After clearing up I made myself a cup of tea and heated some tomato soup. I then slept for an hour but only fitfully as I could hear water dripping into the bilges. I finally stirred myself and found that the water was coming from the hole in the deck where the insulator had been. The best I could do was to fill it with more rags until the weather improved. At 5 p.m. the wind strength was force eight again, but the seas were settling down, and within two hours the barometer had begun to climb. The weather might have improved but I still felt very shaky.

My neck is still sore, and I have a lot of cuts on my hands which sting. I have no willpower to go out on deck and steer and yet if the wind increases to storm force again I shall have to make the effort. The weather must be on the mend even if it's taking a long time.

I awoke the following morning feeling sore and lethargic. I was still heading due north, but making a mere two knots. I didn't dare risk a bigger sail – not yet anyway. With the previous day's decision to sail back to New Zealand still in my mind, I studied the chart and felt an overwhelming depression. All those miles for nothing. Everything I had achieved so far would go to waste. It all seemed so wrong. I sat down and once again wrote out my arguments for giving up, or rather for not going on. The awful indecision was back. As *Crusader* was still in one piece after the previous day's storm, I wasn't sure that my earlier doubts about her seaworthiness in bad weather could still be used as reasons for abandoning my course to Cape Horn. I suddenly began to question my true motives for turning back, and all at once realized that that decision had been caused by fear. How then could I reconsider going on? The answer was that at this precise moment I also realized that by surmounting the storm I had almost totally eliminated the fear that had been dogging me for so long.

In my log I wrote:

a) If that rig can stand a capsize without the proper shrouds, then it should withstand ordinary bad weather when I fit a decent replacement; b) it's 2800 miles to the Falklands as opposed to 3000 to New Zealand against the current and head winds; c) surely there are not likely to be too many severe storms in the next three to four weeks.

Having written down these considerations the decision I had to make became clear: I turned around once more and set course for the Horn. My mood changed rapidly from depression to positive optimism – I was on my way again. I wrote down the priorities for the day:

Fix the hole in the deck where the aerial has broken off.
Make a replacement hatch-cover for the cockpit bin which is open and letting in water.
Fix the shrouds. Yippee! We're off!!

I made reasonably good progress over the next ten days and by 8 March I was 1300 miles from the Horn. I had done all the jobs around the deck and after a total of eleven hours aloft had even succeeded in making a satisfactory repair to the mast. I had discovered, too, that by removing the top seven slides from the reefed mainsail I could hoist the head well above the point where the jury shrouds crossed the track. It wasn't the best arrangement, but for down-wind sailing it was reasonable enough.

Despite all this heartening achievement my mood of elation was shortlived and again I became miserable and depressed.

There is a big sea running from the west, but I can't make real use of the good wind direction as I have no spinnaker pole left to boom-out a jib. I wish I didn't feel so uneasy. If the barometer would rise, so too would my spirits. Progress is quite good but memories of the storm are so vivid that I quake every time I see the signs of a new depression approaching.

I can't see any further than Cape Horn. My thoughts are 'if'
I get there, not 'when'. If I live past the Horn I still have to
clear the Southern Ocean. How I dread this ocean. When I
look at Rob's picture I feel like crying; even he doesn't seem
real any more. My life has narrowed to a single theme –
getting through each day till I round the Horn. The rest of
the world has ceased to have any meaning. This is my entire
life and there is nothing else.

To add to my depression I was also feeling physically unfit at
this time. Possibly the effects of months of relative inactivity
coupled with bursts of excessive hard work were catching up on
me. Although I was eating well, my diet wasn't ideal.

10 March (Day 184)
What extraordinary weather. Pressure's now high although
there's still plenty of wind, lots of work and little sleep. The
unceasing squalls and calms all night require helm adjustments
every half hour or so. It has paid off, though, with another
good run of 120 miles, leaving 1100 miles to the Horn.

On the 12th I wrote:

The high is still around, and so is the wind; I'm now 300
miles from the coast of Chile and will soon have to alter
course south south-east towards the Horn. I'm beginning to
feel a wee twinge of excitement now that the real battle is
about to begin.

I calculated that in terms of sailing time I was just in front of
Chichester's position eleven years earlier, so there was still a
chance for me to 'beat him' round the Horn. However, this
race was seldom uppermost in my mind – more often it was the
race for survival. Chichester had met some of the worst weather
of his trip rounding Cape Horn. He had gone fairly close and of
course the seas are worse there because of the shelving of the
sea bed which creates an additional disturbance. I didn't want
that happening to me and chose to give the Horn a wide berth.
I preferred rather to run the risk of tangling with icebergs than
to catch even a glimpse of the brooding, malignant rock that
was my conception of Cape Horn.

At midnight on 14 March the starboard shrouds collapsed again. I jogged along under shortened sail until morning and then went aloft to inspect the damage. Fortunately, it wasn't too bad. Unable to get the shroud plates over the bolt as originally intended, I had linked them to the bolt with a shackle and a large steel ring. It was the steel ring, gripped by the bolt, which had suffered. The strain must have been immense, for the ring had straightened into an oblong shape before finally parting. I replaced it with a heavy shackle and within half an hour I was on my way again. By mid-day I was 500 miles from the Horn.

On 17 March (Day 191) I took enough careful sights to be sure of my position. I could only trust to luck that the error in my chronometer was remaining constant; it was a predicament that at any other time would have worried me very much, but now I simply minimized the problem and concentrated on more immediate things.

> I feel relieved to have at least one good fix, for, if the weather deteriorates I may not be able to grab another sight for days. The barometer is steady at 998 millibars, which is not too exciting but I'm keeping my fingers crossed. I can still beat Chichester if I keep up this progress.

18 March, 20.00 (Day 192)

> It's bitterly cold on deck. I dressed up intending to watch the sunset but after ten minutes came below, frozen. It's very squally and at times *Crusader* is doing seven knots with just the storm jib and deep reefed main. There is a half moon in the sky which helps. I shall be able to see where I'm going.

Early on the 19th the wind fell away completely and I managed a few hours' sleep, getting up at 2 a.m. when it suddenly blew strongly from the WSW. I kept the mainsail set until 6 a.m., then hauled it down in the increasing wind, disconnected the Sailomat and began to steer. I had planned to pass within fifteen miles to the south (windward) side of Diego Ramirez Islands which lie sixty miles to the west of Cape Horn, but didn't think I would see them unless the visibility improved. It was very cold and it rained all the time. And yet despite the misery I was not too worried about the gale, as I was keyed up for the final battle, and I felt I could tackle anything!

At 4 p.m. I wrote:

> I've steered all day. The wind shows no signs of dropping yet and visibility is still poor, but I must be past the islands by now. I am going to stay on this course until I reckon that I am well past the Horn; then I shall gybe and head for Illa Los Estados on the eastern side. I only hope the wind doesn't force me further south and into the ice. My planned course will take me as much as fifty to sixty miles south of the Horn and that is below the ice limit for this year. The sea pattern has changed, and the waves are now much shorter and steeper which indicates shallower water. *Crusader* is bouncing around like a cork. I'm glad it's no more than just gale force.

In the late evening I gybed towards Illa Los Estados, having estimated I had finally passed Cape Horn, the focal point of all my fears and apprehensions of the previous four months. Then I went to bed at 11.30 and slept for four hours, my longest uninterrupted sleep for six months. When I woke I found myself heading south and hurriedly changed course to the north-east. Curiously enough I didn't think about icebergs, but simply concentrated on coaxing the boat along in the easterly wind and worried about the wind that was increasing rapidly.

Had I but known . . . luck was with me to an incredible degree. The icebergs must have been there all right, but I didn't see them – I didn't look!

At mid-morning the wind increased so I was forced to lie-a-hull; by the afternoon the wind had backed to the SW. Then I continued steering under bare poles for the rest of the afternoon. The wind force was eight with heavy squalls, but by 8 p.m. it had moderated sufficiently for me to put up the storm jib and reconnect the self-steering. I went back to my bunk feeling very tired and absolutely no elation at having passed the Horn.

In fact as I hadn't seen the dreaded rock it might as well not have been there. I wasn't too certain where it was anyway, as I hadn't been able to take sights during the previous three days, and my courses had been so erratic that my dead-reckoning position was little more than a guess. However, I was pretty sure to be over the ice limit and that worried me considerably.

Next day my mood changed:

> I'm past it. Whoopee!! More than that, I'm nearly past Estados! I had the shock of my life when I went up the mast this morning and saw its dim mountains twenty to thirty miles away. My DR after three days was about fifty miles out. Well, nobody's perfect!

I took a sun-sight as soon as I sighted the land and confirmed it as Illa Los Estados, so I broke open a bottle of Riesling, poured a glass and hurled it at the ocean. I had conclusively rounded the old bogey Horn, and I hadn't even laid eyes on it. I may even have been asleep at the time.

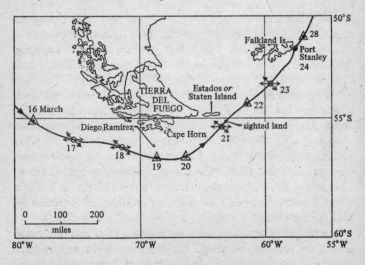

Passage round Cape Horn

14
THE FALKLANDS AND HOMEWARD BOUND

I felt really excited at the thought of reaching the Falklands in a few days and talking to Rob again. I'd never spoken to anyone who'd been to the Falklands, but from the description in the Pilot book it was an interesting place. I was fascinated by the fact that people chose to live in such a remote area and in such an unfavourable climate.

The weather began to improve. It was very cold but quite sunny, and to my prejudiced eye the sea already looked flatter – so it should have been, with South America to buffer the long ocean swell. By the evening of the 21st I was past Estados and right on course for the Falklands – 300 miles away.

I spent the next day feverishly finishing off half-written letters to friends and family, but I was constantly interrupted by a familiar squeaking, and broke off to go on deck. The sea was alive not with the expected dolphins but with leaping pilot whales, hundreds of them. I felt very nervous at first in case they damaged the self-steering rudder, but they seemed to know where they were going. One large whale stood up on his tail with his funny bulbous nose in the air and then sank sublimely back into the deep – goodness knows what he was doing.

I had to cross a shallow bank the following day and this made me rather nervous, although the wind was light and steady. As anticipated the bank had disturbed the wave pattern enormously, so that in this isolated patch the seas were thrown up to nearly twice their normal height. The sudden change seemed sinister and *Crusader* began to pitch and toss in a most unhappy attitude. I disappeared below and washed my hair with extravagant amounts of fresh water – well, I was only half a day from the Falkland Islands, so now it didn't matter.

As I approached the islands, the weather was sunny and clear, but suddenly, as I passed the lighthouse within a mile of the harbour, the wind rose to gale force, and I was forced to lie-a-hull off the entrance. I was quite unable to make for shelter and was rapidly being driven out to sea again. I had radioed my arrival but the contact had been poor, and I wasn't certain whether they had understood. Fortunately, the message had got through and shortly afterwards a powerful-looking fishing vessel arrived to guide me through the narrows; when it became apparent that I was unable to make any headway at all he offered me a tow, which I gratefully accepted – I didn't want to waste valuable time drifting out into the open sea again and having to beat back when the conditions improved.

The Falkland Islands were just as I had imagined them – wind-swept, barren of trees, bleak and with only a scattering of multi-coloured cottages to save them from looking altogether desolate. I saw no saloon cars, but there were a great many Land-Rovers and bicycles; also, to my surprise, there were horses. Most people rode, and in certain parts of the islands horses were the only practical transport.

But the shortcomings the Falklands suffered in terms of weather were more than made up for by the warmth of the people. The customs officer, Les Halliday, for example, had no sooner finished his official business than he invited me to have dinner at home with himself and his wife, Peggy. Then the island's radio operator on his own initiative came to check over my set, to install the new crystals which I had been given in Tasmania but had been unable to fit. Another of the gathering who greeted me noticed the condition of the mast; he immediately said he would talk to the 'chippy' on HMS *Endurance* and see about getting it repaired. The 'chippy', he explained, was a friend of his and the *Endurance* was the navy's Antarctic patrol ship.

Left: In rendezvous position off Tasmania before being directed to shelter

Below: Receiving spares at the rendezvous off Tasmania

Left: My course around Cape Horn

Above: Climbing the mast in Port Stanley was a lot preferable to climbing it in the Southern Ocean

Left: The weeks of strain before Cape Horn take their toll

Far left: Running in front of a severe gale streaming warps

Left: Pounding northwards in the South Atlantic

Right: Crusader steams along with no steering aids

Below: Crusader is sighted in the Western Approaches

Above: The chess pieces I carved with a penknife and screwdriver

Right: I don't think you've combed your hair since I left!

Overleaf: The first step ashore — without a falter!

Left: The minesweeper HMS *Walkerton* sent me over some fresh food for the last few days

Below: The finishing gun!

I was eager to send a message home and was taken to the local telegraph office. It had to be a telegram, I was told, because the island's external telephone lines were only open for two hours a day and not at all on Saturdays and Sundays (this was a Saturday).

That evening I had a long hot bath followed by a superb dinner of roast lamb at the home of Les, the customs man, and his wife. I am not sure which I enjoyed most – the bath, the dinner or their company. How civilized it felt to be sitting down with serviettes, a tablecloth and wine in a glass. And how marvellous fresh meat and vegetables tasted. It was a wonderful feeling and a wonderful evening and made complete for me when a message arrived to say that Rob was home and that he and my family knew that I was safe in the Falkland Islands.

Early next morning, full of energy, I climbed the mast and dismantled my makeshift joinery. The 'chippy' from *Endurance* arrived to help me and took away the broken plates as a pattern for the new set which he promised to have ready by evening.

In the afternoon I had the unique experience of 'talking' to Rob on the telex. I'd never used one before, and watching the typewriter automatically print the words made it seem to me as if it was the machine which was answering my questions, and not Rob. None the less, it was a great thrill, and we arranged a phone call for Monday morning.

That evening the local marine archaeologist invited me to dinner with his friends who included some of the crew of the *Endurance* and the Antarctic supply and research ship *John Biscoe*, which also happened to be in port. Social life on the island seemed to be remarkably lively, perhaps accounted for by the absence of television.

On Sunday the rigging repairs were complete. I was amazed at how quickly the 'chippy' had finished the job and was more than grateful to the crew of *Endurance* for their help. A local firm made a couple of extra mast bolts for me to take, but the general opinion was that the mast was probably stronger now than it had ever been.

Also, now that the new crystals had been installed in the radio

I could hear Portishead quite clearly on the new frequencies.

In the afternoon, accompanied by the *Daily Express* correspondent, John Smith, and his children, I went for a drive to see some penguins. We found some of them hiding in little holes in the dunes by the sea, and they started to make a run for the water. We dashed along the beach to head them off, but I quickly had to stop as my ankles had had virtually no use during the previous months, and were already aching.

It was a beautiful walk along this deserted windswept coast, and I found myself thinking of Rob and wishing we could have been there together. I picked a few pieces of heather to hang over the chart table and remind me of the occasion and my thoughts at that moment.

I had dinner again that night with Les and Peggy; it was a quiet, relaxing evening and the following morning, except for my phone call to Rob, I was all set to go. Rob was waiting for my call and, at the sound of his familiar voice, all the memories and associations of home came rushing back and the Southern Ocean receded into the distance. We had a wonderful chat, and I was delighted to hear that *Great Britain II* had taken the elapsed time prize for the race.

On my return from the post office I found piles of fresh vegetables had been left for me by some kind person. In fact, many people had been bringing me food during my stay on the island, all sorts of things like eggs, cabbages, potatoes, onions and I was generously given the very last of the fruit that had been delivered to the island – a dozen apples and oranges. I'd never seen such kindness.

Something else which impressed me was how versatile the Falkland Islanders were. I came across several who were equally capable as carpenter, radio technician, diver and general handyman; they were amazingly diverse and fiercely independent. There was virtually no crime on the islands and the only vice, I was told, was drink. Well, as I have said before, nobody's perfect.

The weather had deteriorated badly over Sunday and by

Monday morning it looked horrible. The barometer was as low as it had been in the previous storms. If there was a depression coming then I would need plenty of sea room, so it was no use leaving with this threat in the air and being caught so close to the land. The Falklanders were non-committal about the forecast – they'd obviously been wrong before and didn't want to risk telling me anything too encouraging. If I couldn't leave there were many worthwhile things that I could do to make use of the time, and two of my new diving friends were prepared to go down and clean the barnacles off *Crusader*'s hull. I also had an invitation to lunch with the governor of the island and his wife which was a definite honour, and as I had decided to sit out the storm, I accepted.

I had a delicious lunch at the governor's house, and a fascinating conversation with the scientists from the *John Biscoe*. One of their most important research discoveries, they told me, was a little shrimp-like creature called a 'krill' which might in the future be used as a substitute food for the human race. They wanted to find out who or what normally lived off this creature and what would happen if the supply were to become depleted. What diverse occupations people do have!

By the afternoon there was still no change in the weather; the barometer and wind were steady and so, hoping that the weather would make up its mind one way or another overnight, I decided to leave at first light.

Peggy Halliday had put on board some useful items including a big, strong bucket. I had lost or broken three buckets and as substitutes had fixed rope handles to my biggest Tupperware containers. They had been surprisingly satisfactory, but they cracked rather easily and, anyway, I was getting short of them. On finding I was running out of cream crackers she kindly procured a large boxful for me plus some candles, Brasso, scouring powder and some face cream.

I had a last dinner with the Hallidays and went back to *Crusader* early that night, eager to set off in the morning. Just before it got light my alarm rang and Les and Peggy arrived to help me cast off the lines.

By the time I was ready to leave, half a dozen more of my
Falkland Island friends had crowded aboard Port Stanley's
only yacht to accompany me out of the entrance. We sailed
together out of the inner harbour; then, shouting encouragement and waving farewell, they turned and headed back to their
bleak but inwardly warm island which held such fond memories
for me.

Crusader pointed her nose towards the open sea and skimmed
eagerly on past the lighthouse. I had hoisted a reefed mainsail,
staysail and yankee, and in a fresh beam wind she was making a
good six knots. I had called up *Endurance* which had sailed the
previous day and asked them how the weather was to the north
of me. I also called an ice survey vessel, the *Bransfield*, and
received their weather report which included the positions of
several icebergs to the south of me. Icebergs! The mere thought
made me shiver – it was *Endurance* who had told me about the
icebergs near the Horn. How glad I was to be sailing north and
out of the Southern Ocean.

On my second day out from Port Stanley, I was still suffering
from an overdose of 'star treatment'.

30 March (Day 204)
After so long alone it's too easy to be flattered by attention –
I think that I talked too much, showed off and was generally
too conscious that everyone considered me something special.
It makes me feel uncomfortable and Chay's words come to my
mind: 'Never believe your own publicity.' Everyone hates a
big shot, and I hate the thought of becoming one. When I get
home I'll depend on Rob to make sure I keep my feet on the
ground.

On 1 April, I wrote:

It's warm on deck: certainly warm enough to do without
oilskins. Only another 250 miles and I shall officially leave the
Southern Ocean. That will be an event to celebrate! It's hard
to believe that Australia, New Zealand and Cape Horn are

behind me. And oddly enough it is really only the landmarks which I remember, most of the long stretches in between are forgotten like memory blackouts.

I wonder if these past six months have really been well spent, or whether I would have been better off with Rob on *Great Britain II*, or at home? But whatever else I have had six months doing what I like doing – with the exception perhaps of those three weeks when I was approaching the Horn. I've been at ease and happy with myself and free from those headaches and bad dreams which I used to suffer from on land. I wonder if they'll ever come back again, or will this be a permanent cure? Somehow I must work out a solution for my unsociability, or this next year is going to be rather nasty. Rob will help.

How lucky I am to have Rob. He has made this trip possible by giving me peace of mind and is always there to help me in difficult situations; I constantly apply to him for advice. I invite his scorn when I'm stupid, and I can hear his praise when I do things right. I don't need religion, but I certainly need Rob. What a joy it's going to be to return home.

At last it began to feel like spring again. The days were getting warmer and I was able to shut down the cabin heater, put away my woollies, and wear jeans and T-shirts. After months of being covered up I was surprised to find that my once puny arms were now bristling with muscles! And another thing that I uncovered produced a more unpleasant surprise. When I shook out the reef in the mainsail, the bottom third of the sail, almost permanently furled in a reef, had a harvest of mould upon it. Muscles and mould! Amazing the things which continue to grow in winter.

I made contact with my old friend Portishead Radio on 2 April and had another long talk to Rob. He and Chay were now busy with the new boat, *Great Britain IV*, which they were building for the Round Britain Race in July. It all sounded very exciting, but Rob encouraged me not to dwell on these coming events, but to concentrate on getting home as soon as possible – he was tired of washing his own shirts!

The wind, boisterous and sometimes squally, stayed with me, but progress was excellent and once again I estimated that I had covered just under 1000 miles that week.

6 April (Day 211)
I intended calling *Endurance* this evening but there is so much lightning in the sky that I'm frightened to try. I love thunderstorms on land, but out here it's a different thing altogether.

I was able to swap my paperbacks in Port Stanley and so now I have plenty to read in the evenings, but some nights I just sit by the light of a candle and dream about Rob and our home.

On the 11th, Day 216, the wind was lighter, with further squalls – rather like the Doldrums. I found a flying fish on the deck in the morning. He was small so I threw him overboard although I planned to eat his big brother when he came aboard.

I had managed to make 125 miles a day from the Falkland Islands – the best average speeds of the trip over an equivalent distance. I no longer had to slow down on account of the self-steering gear or worry about the mast – thanks to the Sailomat and the 'chippy' from *Endurance*. I was pleased to find that, since rounding the Horn – not counting the delay of three and a half days in the Falkland Islands – Chichester had only gained a day's sailing on me. I'd rounded the Horn one day ahead of him, and if I could keep up an average of 110 miles a day from here I should beat his record – assuming, of course, no unforeseen disasters. I was, in fact, having further trouble with the main rudder about this time. It was getting almost too stiff to be of use, and I was relying entirely on the Sailomat for steerage.

My poor hands were suffering from misuse, and the skin on them was peeling, even though I always wore sailing gloves when practicable and liberally rubbed them with cream every day. My fingers looked like tiny snakes shedding their skin, and my nails were white and peculiar. I read that the same thing had happened to Marilyn Bailey who had been adrift with her husband in a liferaft for 118 days. Evidently it was a type of dermatitis caused by long immersion in sea water.

The three days until 17 April witnessed a succession of poor runs; this cut my average back considerably and I lost a whole day to Chichester. The wind had died and obviously I had reached the area of calm called the Variables. I tried not to concern myself unduly, and filled my time cleaning the ship. I washed the walls and deck head in the cabin and rubbed away the thick green weed from the waterline. To do this I had to lean over the side and hang on by my toes, something I never attempted without double-checking my safety harness! That evening rain fell, pitting the surface of the sea which was as flat and shiny as glass. In the west a bonfire of crimson and gold reflected across the water and on to the sails. 'Oh, well,' I wrote in my log, 'who's in a hurry? Enjoy the peace; it won't last for ever.'

I continued spring cleaning on and off over the next few days and began to get rather annoyed at a load of little house flies which were multiplying in great style. I didn't have any fly spray and didn't know how to get rid of them. I tried treating them to an orgy of pale dry sherry in the hope they would either asphyxiate themselves or drown; but it seems I only succeeded in intoxicating them, for they bred merrily on. (Pale sherry is clearly an aphrodisiac.)

During one of the intervals between 'house' work sessions I called Juliet in Vienna and was delighted to hear she would be producing a baby Austrian in October. She and her husband, Heini, would be coming to Dartmouth for my arrival which, according to Rob, would be on 7 June. I was overjoyed to hear that my parents would also be there. They were taking a four-month holiday in Europe. 'Things are happening!' I noted in my log.

On the 25th I came up on deck in the morning and gaped in surprise at a ship about two miles away on an intercepting

course. I went down below again in a hurry to clothe myself and
watched her from the cockpit. A mile away she altered course
and passed half a mile under my stern. Her name was *Gherania*,
but I couldn't tell where she came from; she was the first vessel
I'd seen since Australia.

26 April (Day 231)

While sitting in the bow this morning waiting to take the
noon-sight I was watching *Crusader* slip through the water and
marvelling at the power that moves her. Her sails are filling
under the gentle breeze, and they seem to be placed in just the
right position to propel her at maximum efficiency. I'm glad I
haven't a scientific turn of mind, or I am sure it would spoil
what for me is pure magic. Today I can't worry about anything.
There is a perfect combination of sunshine, sparkling blue sea
and a breeze soft enough to fan away the heat. A day for doing
favourite things like cleaning the brass on the compass,
sextant, wheel and chronometer; what a wonderful colour
brass is.

This is a day for being aware of the joy of living. It doesn't
matter if I fall into a fit of rage tomorrow because of the lack
of wind. Today will stamp itself indelibly on my mind as the
highest point of my nine months' journey. Soon I shall be
returning to my real or normal life, but the peace and
harmony of this interlude will stay in my mind and no doubt
encroach upon my *real* life in, as yet unforeseen, ways. I now
know, without question, that I can live without the attraction
of society, which is both good and bad. I see no merit in
'opting out' and becoming a recluse, and I feel it is right for
me to accept the social world for what it is and to live with it.
It doesn't matter so long as one's values and ethics remain
intact. And in taking occasional interludes away from the rest
of the world I will always have a tried and tested way of
building up my reserves.

My flying fish's little brother arrived on deck one morning –
all of three-quarters of an inch long. A high flyer for such a
little fella.

On 30 April, Day 235, I slipped back across the equator and

into the Northern Hemisphere without really taking much
notice of it. The trade winds came and blew strongly until
1 May when, to my disappointment, they fizzled out again.
For the next few days I ghosted along at two knots with the
usual sail-flapping and clanking of blocks. Added to this noise
was the loud chirping of two young birds making a fuss about
something. It was an unfamiliar sound, as the birds of the
Southern Ocean had been the silent type.

2 May (Day 237)
How quickly conditions can change! I take back all those
nasty things I said about the Tilley lamp. It made a fine storm
lamp last night in the rain and spray, and remained alight in
the force seven wind.

But that was last night: now it's calm again. I'm weary of
all these changing winds, gales one minute and calms the next.
I am bored too of all the sail changes that are required and
sick of the continuous mental effort required to get up and
make those changes and keep the boat moving. I feel that I
have had just about all I can take of the varying conditions
which have dogged me all the trip. At the moment I have had
enough of sailing – eight months of it seems about as much as
I can manage. But willing or not, I cannot give up unless I
wish to remain a permanent feature of the North Atlantic.
Radio and batteries are working well so I'm making more calls,
especially to Rob. I shall see him before I reach England as he
is coming out to the Azores with the newspaper and TV
crews. I have mixed feelings about this meeting with Rob
because he is not allowed on board and must therefore remain
at arm's length. However, I'm looking forward to it, and it
spurs me on to greater efforts; they say every mile counts
treble in this area.

By that evening I knew I'd reached the Doldrums and it was
alarming – hours of furious squalls, thunderstorms and driving
rain during one of the blackest nights I'd ever seen. Towards daylight the wind fell away and four hours later it rose again from
the NE. This was the signal that I was through the Doldrums.
I was amazed to be clear so quickly, and for a while I couldn't
believe it, but the NE 'trades' definitely were there to stay.

For the next two weeks until 15 May I enjoyed tremendous sailing. The days were somehow all alike, the same wind strength and direction, mottled sunshine and spray, and *Crusader* pounding northwards unceasingly.

I was delighted when the dolphins made their reappearance at dusk one day. I saw them coming at a distance on the beam, hundreds of them, racing full tilt towards me and leaping out of the waves to incredible heights; they would twist in the air, falling on their sides and into the water with a mighty splash. When they reached the yacht they turned about and, matching my modest six knots, kept station, weaving back and forth through the bow wave, their grey bodies sleek and as fat as butter. Standing on the bow I watched two of them moving in perfect unison; noses and tails swaying to and fro, till I thought I was seeing double. I read that Chichester sometimes frightened them off when he made a sudden movement or noise, but these fellows were nothing like so timid. Waving my arms in greeting and yelling at the top of my voice seemed to encourage and provoke them to greater frivolity and squeaking. I left the deck soon afterwards to escape the heat, but for a long while I heard them continuing to play around the boat.

Shortly before dark I went to examine the self-steering and found the rudder blade had snapped in half. It had broken through the thick of the blade, obviously as the result of contact with a heavy object – heavier, I would have thought, than a dolphin. I put on the spare and was faced with a real worry, for if this one broke I would have none left and no main steering. The helm was so stiff by then that it was virtually unusable.

On the last call to Rob, he had suggested that if we lost radio contact I should make for Ponte Delgarde in the Azores, where he would wait for me. It turned out to be a wise suggestion for on the next call I found my transmitter out of action. I was heading for Ponte Delgarde anyway but still felt rather apprehensive and annoyed at being out of contact at such a crucial time. I wanted to tell him that I had been making much better speeds since I had last spoken to him five days earlier, but perhaps it would be premature to advance my ETA as it was still 700 miles to the Azores.

To keep my mind off the rudder, the radio, and potential catastrophes, I once again tidied the boat. This time I checked my remaining provisions. In fact, I found that I would have been able to survive comfortably on the leftovers for another year, so generous had Philip been.

After two weeks' idleness the winches on the starboard side had seized up. I had remained on starboard tack while in the 'trades', so they never came into use. I freed all but the last winch, but that one had a rusted allen screw which I couldn't undo. I was exasperated. I had to get it off or the winch was useless, so I cut a slot in the top of the screw with a hacksaw. But it still wouldn't turn, and by the time I had to admit defeat the screw looked as though it had had a serious accident. I stared balefully at a ship passing half a mile away and wondered what all those smart males aboard might have suggested. Then I tried to remove the winch drum with the rusted screw still in it, and, much to my surprise, I succeeded. Now that's what I call an efficiently designed piece of equipment, I thought to myself. I cleaned it up, put it back and once again had it running freely. I even forgave the crew of that ship for their superior attitude.

By the 15th I had lost the trade winds.

15 May (Day 250)

The wind is now blowing feebly from São Miguel, the place I'm heading for. I could keep up a reasonable day's run by staying on the one tack, but that would take me either to the east or to the north and neither would bring me much closer to the island. I'm in the shipping lanes again and weary from lack of sleep. My dreams, always prolific, are now positively inspiring; and every time I wake I muse over the dream I've interrupted. Mostly they concern sailing; I get washed up on the beach several times a night, and last night the self-steering broke and I saw to my horror all the bits trailing in the wake. I woke from that pretty quick and ran to the stern to make sure it was only a dream!

Every night I listen to the Portishead traffic list, and on the 15th I was rewarded with a message: 'Skipper, *Express Crusader*,' the operator read. 'If convenient, rendezvous Ponte Delgarde 37°30N 25°40W. We shall keep visual VHF and 2182 watch from 20 to 25 May. Signed, Rob.' Oh, if only my transmitter were working I could reply and tell him I will be there!

The next ten days turned out to be the most frustrating of my life.

18 May (Day 253)
Now that I want to push on as much as I can the weather has become maddeningly perverse. The wind is light and fitful and this means for me a dead beat to windward. The last three days' runs have been less than eighty miles each. I was becalmed for five hours in the early morning and I hoped the wind might appear from the west, but no such luck.

Oh, these Horse latitudes! If I had any horses on board I'd put them between the shafts. My poor wooden knights are a-quivering in the bottom of their box. Maybe something is going to happen, though. There's a definite feel of the higher latitudes in the air, and today I am chilly in my track suit. Yesterday I was stretched out in the sun in the altogether. As of noon, 560 miles to São Miguel.

My log on the 22nd at 17.00 read:

If the weather doesn't change soon I'll go barmy; whatever the wind, it is always heading me. I've never felt so desperate and frustrated. Only sixty miles to the rendezvous, but it is going to be the longest sixty miles of the voyage.

23 May (Day 258) At last:

Land again; it's the island of St Maria in the Azores. What a struggle this has been – and looks like continuing to be – to make the next few miles to the rendezvous. Still, there's no point in hurrying now, because darkness will set in soon, and I can't make the rendezvous till daylight.

To my alarm I then heard a noise like a ship approaching, loud and very close. A few seconds passed, and out of the mist appeared an old naval aircraft, just a few hundred feet above the water and going quite slowly. It flew right over my head and then disappeared into the mist. Rather puzzled, I wrote in my log: 'Fancy that plane flying over so low; I hope there's nothing wrong with it.'

By the evening of the 23rd I could see the faint outline of São Miguel, and the wind was just free enough to allow me to sail there on a direct course. I arrived off the entrance at 9 p.m. It was already dark and so I hove-to and prepared to spend the night drifting.

At midnight I was going up on deck for a check and saw a boat quite close and heading straight towards me. I was diving below to start the engine to get out of its way when I heard a shout. I would have known that voice anywhere! There was a searchlight shining on me, and I could see a mass of figures running around the deck. Then I heard a concerned shout: 'Turn that damn light out of her eyes!' Yes, it was Rob all right!

15
RENDEZVOUS AT SEA

We yelled to each other across the gap between the two boats –
Rob asked me if I wanted to go straight on or whether I would
wait around until daylight. I called back that I would wait till
morning, so Rob suggested I follow them into sheltered water.

Two hours later I was alongside the trawler and received a
big hug – difficult even with the two hulls so close together, but
marvellous just the same. I was then introduced to the television
film crew. Rob had convinced them that I would turn up on
time, although he hadn't been able to convince the *Daily
Express*, for whom the rendezvous was arranged, and they had
decided not to come; 'disbelievers!' There was so much to talk
about; Rob and I stayed talking on our respective decks till
dawn broke, and we still didn't get through all the questions we
both wanted to ask each other. As soon as it was light enough,
the filming was done, and I reluctantly said good-bye to Rob
again.

It was still another 1200 miles to Dartmouth and the longer I
delayed the harder it was going to be to face them, so I let go
the trawler's lines and got under way. I was then accompanied
to the open sea, where the wind started to pick up. My heart
twinged as I saw Rob waving good-bye from the deck, and I
thought of the things that could happen between now and seeing
him again. Just one final effort was needed and the journey
would be over. I simply had to avoid ships and the odd navigational hazard and I would be home. That's what I told myself
as I had a last glimpse of Rob and wearily started the long beat
down to the end of the island.

I was exhausted by nightfall. The excitement of seeing Rob

and chatting with him through the night, followed by a hard
day of windward sailing, had had their effect. Yet I had to stay
awake and keep a lookout for ships. Rob had brought me a
portable transmitter, arranged and lent by Racal, and I was able
to call the *Daily Express* and give my ETA. As Rob pointed out,
I should be home on 8 June, even allowing for adverse weather,
and that would still be two days within Chichester's time. Rob
told me there were plans to celebrate my arrival, and they
sounded fantastic.

Conditions were calm for three days and I was about to delay
the ETA, but the wind finally arrived – and how! On 28 May,
Day 262, my day's run was an amazing 170 miles – one of the
best. By 30 May I had a little over 600 miles left to cover, and I
was now using the chart which showed the area from Gibraltar
to the UK. Wayward ships remained my only obstacle – the
one hazard that stood between me and home – and I turned to
the old routine of sleeping for just half an hour at a time. Radio
contact with Rob was poor, but I learnt that a rendezvous was
planned to take place 100 miles from Dartmouth, in a position
40 miles south of Land's End on the evening of the 5th.

1 June (Day 266)
Last night while on deck two small fluffy birds flew up and
made a frenzied attempt to land on deck. They first thought
the mainsail was the best spot, but couldn't get a grip on it.
They appeared to find my presence more encouraging and
several times tried to land on me – one momentarily clung on
to a crease in my oilskin jacket. Eventually, one of them
found a perch on the mainsail winch on the mast, and the
other squatted out of the wind behind a genoa winch in the
cockpit. They looked as though they were there to stay and
certainly my presence didn't disturb them. Then around
midnight the wind died down. I should have shaken the reef
out of the main, but with a bird on the winch desperately
in need of sleep, how could I be heartless enough to disturb
him? I left it until 2.30 a.m., but then had to take some action
as *Crusader* had almost stopped. I went forward and looked at

the bird in the torch light. He was asleep, swaying gently back
and forth with the rhythm of the boat, and when I touched
him his feathers were cold, but I was pleased to find his little
body felt warm. As I lifted him from his perch he gave a
horrible squawk and began to wriggle, but he quietened down
when I put him into the open cockpit locker. I took out the
reef and later shone my torch in the locker and found him
fast asleep.

At dawn both birds were still sleeping like untidy pieces of
thistle down, their eyes tight shut and oblivious to the world.
At 7 a.m. they had gone.

I was desperately afraid of being run down by a ship and kept
watch as best I could, but lack of sleep was nevertheless making
me careless, and on the evening of 1 June I had a very close
shave. I was lying in my bunk listening to the wind, wondering
whether to reef, when something made me start and I jumped
up to see a ship approaching fast and looming large on the
starboard bow. Fortunately, I didn't have to tack to avoid it
but simply bore away and pointed the boat at its stern. Its close
proximity shook me as it steamed past, and seconds later
Crusader was hit by its wash which caused her to roll violently
and take water over the decks. Quite illogically I was *not*
particularly upset by the event; statistically, I felt it must reduce
the chances of something like this happening again. I put great
store by my special interpretation of the law of probabilities.

2 June (Day 267)
I feel so restless. Although I'm only 100 miles from England I
cannot raise anyone on the radio. Portishead can hardly hear
me, and I can't get any answer from Land's End Radio. It is
so frustrating because I really do feel like talking to someone
now. I'll try Portishead later; perhaps it will be better after
dark.

It's a good thing I have three days in which to reach the
rendezvous because I am now doing one knot in the wrong
direction! I've seen a number of ships today, so I'll have to
keep a better lookout tonight. I have to shine a torch on
Crusader's sails to signal my presence to other boats because
my navigation lights are no longer working.

Despite some negative speeds and only average overall progress it was now obvious that I was going to arrive at the rendezvous point far too early. By the evening of 2 June I was only forty miles away. Yet I didn't want to advance the ETA because I feared that the elaborate preparations being made on my behalf would be wrecked if I showed up too soon. It simply wasn't fair to upset the organizers at this late stage, and I realized that I was no longer in a hurry. The urgency I'd felt throughout the voyage had suddenly evaporated, leaving me curiously devoid of feeling, and I wanted to give myself time to assimilate the fact that what I'd attempted was finished. Combined with this was a sort of reluctance to face the crowds and the fuss in Dartmouth. I could have slipped in unseen but, of course, that would have disappointed a lot of people, and after all that my family and friends had gone through it would have been a sneaky thing to do.

On the morning of the 3rd, as I approached the rendezvous area, another large aeroplane passed low overhead. I wondered if it was trying to avoid the cloud layer. I thought it might have been a DC8 but my knowledge of plane breeds is scant, and it could just as easily have been a Sopwith Camel. I gave the pilots a wave as it passed over, but I didn't think they saw me. It was flying only a couple of hundred feet above the sea, and I felt a thrill at seeing another creature so close.

A few miles short of the rendezvous point I took the sails down and drifted; I had two days to wait. Visibility was poor although the wind had died and it was quiet. I opened the hatches, hoping in this way to hear any approaching ships without constantly having to go out on deck to look for them. I finished touching up some bits of varnish in the saloon and worked for a few hours on my chess pieces. I noticed one of my poor bishops had a crack which looked as if it might get worse – the crack ran from his chin through his nose and down the back of his hat. Obviously he needed first aid, so I drilled a hole in the side of his head and nailed him together. That fixed him except that the nail head stuck out like a sore thumb. I put him back in his box and promised him proper surgery when I got home.

Secretly I wondered if I would ever have the time and the patience to repair him or even complete the set – after hours and hours I'd only carved sixteen pieces which is, of course, only half a set.

In the evening I sat at the chart table, sipping a sweet martini and watching the light disappearing from the sky. *Crusader* rolled gently in the swell, and the quiet was only disturbed by the constant crack and rattle of blocks and the soft lapping of waves against the hull. It was strange to be motionless after so long, and even stranger not to feel frustrated by the lack of progress. From my seat at the chart table I looked affectionately around the boat and wondered at the faith I'd put in the sturdy ten-year-old hull. I had such confidence in her now that I was sure she could take me all the way round again without a falter. Could I have found a better, more trustworthy, capable boat? I wondered. No, I doubt it, even if I'd looked for years.

I thought again about the other single-handers and wondered about their various motives and incentives. Were their motives the same as mine? Who knows? But there was one thing we all had in common and that was having a good boat, sufficient knowledge to keep ourselves out of trouble, and faith.

That evening I wrote in my journal on this subject:

Robin Knox-Johnson was only partially right when he said, 'a man would have to be inhumanly confident and self-reliant to make this sort of trip without faith in God' – but there are other kinds of faith. Faith is security, and I get my security from my background, from Rob and from my family and my friends. With these I am never alone. Whether I see them or not, they are a part of my mind and just as infallible a source of comfort and strength to me as God must be to a believer. Faith does not mean an expectation of miracles. I don't really believe that anyone in a storm-tossed boat would expect God to calm the waves. What he might ask for is help to fortify his mind and to endure. The strength of faith is in the believer; regardless of what his faith is based upon – and I imagine that there is very little difference between the attitudes of Chay, Chichester, Knox-Johnson or myself – we

call upon our reserves of faith and willpower and hope that it
will see us through. While struggling for two hours up the mast
trying to undo the nut that had seized I had said to myself,
'You'll just *have* to get the damn thing off!' And finally, using
brute strength I didn't know I had, the nut started to yield.
My background provided me with the will to persevere, and it
was the knowledge that it was up to me alone to free the nut
that provided the strength.

After my noon-sights on 4 June, Day 269, I found I had
drifted ten miles east of the rendezvous point, so I got under way
and sailed leisurely back towards it. It was raining and there
was thick black cloud above, but the wind was moderate. If it
held it would blow me home nicely, I noted. I hove-to at the
rendezvous and cooked myself a meal.

I spent the entire morning of 5 June trying to contact Land's
End Radio but with no success. Eventually the motor boat
Fleur answered and kindly obliged me with a link to the radio
station. I was told that Rob, together with reporters and photographers, would be leaving Penzance on the trawler *Pathfinder*
at noon and would be in my area by 6 p.m.

I took more sights and found that I'd drifted to the west, so
I set sail and headed in a direction which I hoped would inter-
cept the rendezvous trawler.

By 6 p.m. I was frantic; there was not a vessel in sight and yet
I was absolutely certain I was in the right position. Well, that
is to say I was certain until Land's End Radio told me that my
signal strength sounded as if I was still in the Bay of Biscay! But
just as awful doubts started creeping into my mind I overheard
Rob talking to Land's End Radio. He sounded gloomy and was
reporting that the trawler had developed engine failure and
would have to be towed into Falmouth. Hoping I would be
listening in, he said he wouldn't be able to make the rendezvous
that night but would find some way to get out to me in the
morning. In the meantime he suggested I should close the coast.
Poor Rob, he never did have much luck with engines.

Well, that explained why I couldn't spot the advance welcom-
ing party, but it still didn't explain why I couldn't see England.

By my calculations I was supposed to be only twenty miles away!
I sailed towards the point where I thought the Lizard light
should be and climbed the mast to look for it. It was drizzling,
visibility was poor and the horizon ahead was piled sky-high
with masses of black cloud; I desperately willed to it transform
itself into the friendly green coast of England, but needless to say
it obstinately refused. I sailed another five miles, and as the dusk
gradually began to mute the edges of the clouds I climbed the
mast again and peered ahead. Minutes passed and then in the
corner of my eye I saw what I was looking for. A flash, then
another, and another; the Lizard light – I had found it! I was so
relieved and excited that I shot down the mast and danced
around the deck yelling at the top of my voice.

16
JOURNEY'S END

The shipping was quite heavy in the lane which ran between me and the Lizard, so as I didn't want to stay up all night on look-out I took the sails down and stayed where I was. Feeling tired by this time I fell asleep for two hours. On waking I amused myself by counting the ships as they steamed past and guessing what cargoes they carried. Then, when I was sufficiently drowsy again I opened the hatches, went to bed and slept intermittently through the rest of the night.

At 6.30 a.m. I hoisted sail and headed towards the coast. The wind was light and the tide was against me so the going was abysmally slow. At 10.30 a.m. while unsuccessfully trying to call Rob at home, Land's End Radio told me the minesweeper HMS *Walkerton* was approaching me with Rob on board. I had hardly replaced the handset on the radio when to my great surprise I saw the *Walkerton* only fifty yards away! Her captain, Lieutenant Alan Adair, had heard of the trawler's engine trouble and had sailed off from Dartmouth immediately, picking up Rob on the way. I was taken aback by the sounds of 'Land of Hope and Glory' coming from the ship's loudspeakers, accompanied by much cheering and waving. Rob was on the bridge with a funny look on his face I had to dive below for a moment to blow my nose!

When I reappeared, a boat was being launched and soon Rob, the *Daily Express* photographers, reporters and ITN crew were alongside. I thought Rob looked very comical in a half-inflated lifejacket – navy regulations insist on lifejackets for passengers in rubber dinghies. We tried to speak but our words were drowned by the sound of a helicopter overhead which, it transpired, had a package for me from 771 Naval Air Squadron at Culdrose. The squadron's gift to me was a shield wrapped up in an airsick bag – and I appreciated them both! Then the captain of the *Walkerton* sent over a present of the ship's crest together with a box of fresh bread and eggs. It was an extremely nice gesture, and I was delighted with the fresh food.

Shortly after 11.30 the trawler *Pathfinder* joined us and Rob and the press transferred to her. As the *Walkerton* prepared to leave, the crew fired rockets and the captain promised to escort me into Dartmouth on the 8th.

By mid-day the excitement was over for the moment. The wind was very light and dead astern so I put up the ghoster and slowly drifted with the tide past the Lizard and into Falmouth Bay, while *Pathfinder* remained in attendance. Rob talked to me on the VHF and took over the navigation.

As I passed the Lizard I received a message of congratulations from the coastguard and lighthouse keepers. I thanked them profusely, remembering that I'd never been so happy to see anything in my life as that light on the Lizard.

I felt pleasantly tired but very happy as I cruised along the coast. Nothing could go wrong now that Rob was going to watch over me during the night and warn me of any approaching ships. I had absolutely no worries. I would much rather have had him aboard of course but I was determined to go along with the rules of single-handed sailing, even though they seemed rather silly at this late stage. In fact there are no hard and fast rules attached to single-handed voyages of this sort; it is just accepted that one imposes one's own discipline. Being towed, and allowing people on board are, for example, both considered unacceptable for a single-handed trip. And, of course, no engines except when manoeuvring.

At lunchtime *Pathfinder* was slightly to windward of me and I noticed an enticing smell of cooking coming from her galley. Someone on board must have realized how this was affecting me for the skipper himself came over in the dinghy with a plate of delicious roast beef, cooked by himself, he told me.

I sailed on until midnight and then hove-to about ten miles south of Plymouth. We had only about sixty miles left to the finishing line and a whole day and a half in which to do it, so with my faithful watchkeeper near at hand I was able to sleep soundly for the rest of the night.

Pathfinder left me for a few hours in the morning to land the film crew in Plymouth, and I spent the time sandpapering my chess pieces and listening to the local radio station. When she returned I hoisted sail and we set off to Start Point. It was very misty and the coastline was only discernible at a distance of two miles. *Crusader* sailed beautifully along the coast, and I was intensely proud of her. I sat on the coach roof in my oilskins and laughed at Rob trying to take a photograph of her from the wet bow of the trawler.

Rob was still taking photographs when the skipper called him to the bridge. He disappeared for a while, then re-emerged and called across the water, 'Do you want to open the Southampton Boat Show?'

Startled, I replied that I should love to, and he went inside the bridge to give my reply to the organizer. How extraordinary, I thought, and tried to imagine what my life would be like from now on. How would it feel being surrounded by people again? How would I take to giving talks and explaining why I made the journey? Then a thought came to my rescue; it was something I'd worked out for myself a long time ago in order to overcome shyness and the fear of talking to people whether singly or in groups. I had convinced myself that it made no difference whether I was being watched by a hundred people or just one, since each had only one pair of eyes and one pair of ears and each was a human being like me. Each was just as much on his own as me.

Nothing had changed. Rob was just across the water, looking and acting exactly as he had always done; although I had never had any doubts, it was wonderful falling straight back into our old relationship, with no strangeness or shyness between us.

We anchored that night under the Devon hills, a few miles southwest of Dartmouth. In the morning it was calm and clear as I hoisted sail for the last time and headed towards Dartmouth. I saw a boat approaching and as it came closer I saw a familiar face waving from the bow. Alexandra! She had come to cheer me in with a mass of friends and we laughed and shouted our greetings; then suddenly I thought it important for me to look presentable so I dived below to wash my hair. When I came up on deck with my hair dripping wet there were half a dozen other boats approaching. Rob called out to me to say that we should gybe for the entrance. It was now 8 a.m. and I was due to cross the line at 9.15. The wind was light and we still had seven miles to go so I was getting anxious about whether we should make it. More and more boats came out from the river and I watched them in amazement, desperately trying to dry my hair in the feeble sunlight. Half an hour later boats completely encircled me.

Finally, *Walkerton* appeared and escorted me towards the river entrance. I became dizzy turning my head in so many directions. I was waving at people in boats all around me but not really seeing their faces. One boat came in particularly close and I greeted its occupants without recognizing them. Then suddenly I heard what sounded like an agonized cry and I froze in disbelief. It was the voice of my mother! I saw then that both my parents were aboard, along with Juliet and Heini. We laughed and yelled at each other but it was quite impossible to hear above the noise of boats' sirens and whistles. Rob signalled to me that I should alter course again to allow for the tide, and for a brief moment I concentrated on the direction in which I was supposed to be heading. We were quite close to the entrance and there was a helicopter overhead adding to the din. Rob shouted that I was approaching the line, but I could see nothing except a sea of boats and waving people. I looked around again for Rob and saw that he had his arm lifted and he was pointing in the direction of the finishing gun. Suddenly as the gun exploded my heart leapt and I yelled an exalted hooray, which was matched a thousand times by the cheers and sirens from the surrounding boats. Somehow, above the racket I

heard Rob say, 'Pull the sails down,' and I ran forward un-
steadily to let go the main and jib halyards and drop the sails on
the deck. I shut my eyes for a moment and then turned round.
A few seconds later Rob's arms were around me.

In attempting this voyage I risked losing a life that had at last
become fulfilling; but in carrying it out I experienced a second
life, a life so separate and complete it appeared to have little
relation to the old one that went before. I feel I am still much
the same person now, but I know that the total accumulation of
hours and days of this voyage have enriched my life immeasurably.

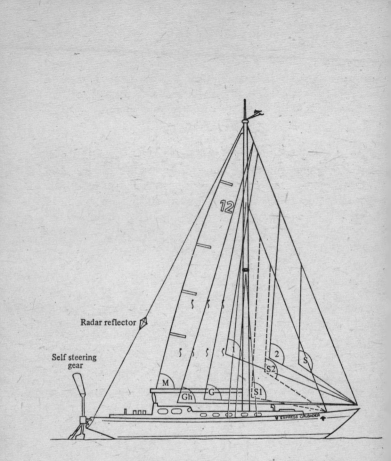

Radar reflector

Self steering gear

All sails used:—

M — Mainsail
Gh — Ghoster
G — Genoa
1 — No.1 Yankee

2 — No.2 Yankee
S — Storm jib
S1 — No.1 Staysail
S2 — No.2 (or storm) Staysail

Also carried but not used:—

2 spare mainsails
2 special downwind genoas

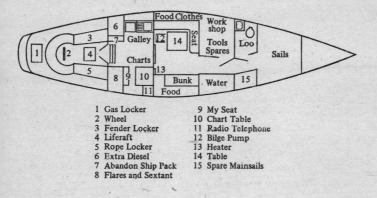

1 Gas Locker
2 Wheel
3 Fender Locker
4 Liferaft
5 Rope Locker
6 Extra Diesel
7 Abandon Ship Pack
8 Flares and Sextant

9 My Seat
10 Chart Table
11 Radio Telephone
12 Bilge Pump
13 Heater
14 Table
15 Spare Mainsails

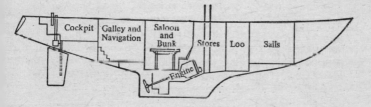

Length overall 53 feet   Waterline length 38 feet 9 inches
Beam 13 feet   Displacement 15 tons
Draft 7 ft 6 inches   Sail area 1500 square feet

Designer E. G. VAN de STADT

Builder Tyler Boat Co. and Southern Ocean Shipyard (1968)

GLOSSARY

Abeam: (bearing) An object is said to be abeam when it is at a right angle to the centre line of the yacht.

Amplitude: Name given to an exercise for determining the error of the compass by taking a bearing of a rising/setting sun and referring to the 'amplitude' tables.

Antifouling: Paint applied to underside of the boat which contains poisons to kill weeds, barnacles etc.

Beam: Width of the boat.

Beating to windward; or 'a beat': A yacht cannot sail directly into the wind and thus if her destination lies upwind this can only be reached by sailing a succession of 'tacks' or zigzag courses each about 45° from the direction of the wind.

Bilge: The very curved part of the boat's hull beneath the water where it turns in towards the keel. In common use and as used within this book the term implies the whole of the area above the keel and under the floorboards where all the water collects.

Block: Sea term for a pulley.

Boom: Metal spar running horizontally from the mast to which the bottom of the mainsail (foot) is attached.

Boomed-out: A genoa or jib can be held on the opposite side to the mainsail when running by rigging a boom (usually a spinnaker boom) from the mast in such a way that it holds the sail out to catch the wind.

Boom-vang: A tackle that prevents the boom from rising and also from swinging inboard.

Bosun's chair: Sling chair suspended from a halyard and used for working aloft.

Broach: To go out of control when running before the wind and sea; it invariably results in the boat being turned sideways and laid over, which leaves her vulnerable for the next wave.

Capsize: To overturn.

Chain plates: Metal plates or straps which are bolted to the sides of the boat or through the deck to carry the lower end of the shrouds which in turn support the mast.

Cleat: A fitting to which a rope can be made fast.

Close hauled: All sails sheeted in hard, i.e. the boat is sailing into the wind.

Cockpit: The sunken well at the aft or end of the boat where the steering wheel and compass are situated, i.e. the area where the helmsman and crew usually sit.

Comber: Large breaking wave.

Dead reckoning: An estimated position of where the boat is thought to be with only course (direction) and speed taken into account.

Forestay: Wire support which runs from top of mast to bow. The foresails are secured to the forestay.

Galley: Boat's kitchen.

Genoa: Large foresail which overlaps the mainsail.

Ghoster: Light weather genoa of large area and light material.

Go about (or tack): To turn the boat's head through the wind in order to sail with the wind on the opposite side, i.e. the necessary change in direction when beating to windward.

Goose-wing: See 'Boomed-out'.

Guy: A rope which is used to support a boom or a spar to check its movement.

Gybe: When the wind is blowing from astern, the mainsail is set at right angles to catch the maximum wind. If the helmsman is not careful or there is a sudden wind shift then the sail may be blown to the opposite side with such violence that damage may result; this is known as the 'accidental gybe'. Alternatively a 'controlled gybe' is a way to change direction by putting the boat's stern through the wind instead of having to turn fully about to put the head through the wind. An intended gybe requires good timing and fast action and even then is rarely attempted in strong winds.

Halyard: Rope or wire with which a sail is hoisted.

Headsail: Another term for foresail.

Heave-to: To stop the boat by setting the headsail and mainsail in opposite sides so that their resultant forces are nullified. The wheel is usually lashed upwind.

Jib: Small foresail.

Knockdown: Boat laid over by a wave until her mast is horizontal, or further.

Lee-cloth: Strip of canvas which can be secured down the edge of a bunk to prevent the occupant falling out.

Lee shore: Shore towards which the wind is blowing. In strong winds frequently dangerous for a sailing yacht which may be pressed on to the shore and unable to get clear because of its inability to sail directly into the wind.

Lee side: Side opposite to which the wind is blowing.

Lifeline: Stout line rigged on deck for the safety of crew in bad weather, or a personal line attached to a safety harness which can be clipped to any strong point.

Log: Abbreviation for log book which is a diary of events; usually of navigational significance.

Luff: The leading edge of a sail; to luff (vb) is to steer closer into the wind.

Lying-a-hull: To take down all sail and allow the boat to wallow. She will lie beam on to the seas.

Parallel rules: An instrument used for laying courses and bearings on a chart, it comprises two rulers joined by hinged arms.

Pitching: The up and down movement of a boat moving across waves.

Pounding: The impact of the underside of the boat striking a wave. It is uncomfortable and in extreme cases can cause damage.

Quarter: (bearing) An object is on the quarter when it lies between the beam and the stern.

Reef: To reduce the amount of mainsail area in strong winds by rolling or folding down and tying its bottom edge (foot).

Rhumb-line: A line on the surface of the world that cuts parallels of latitude at equal angles. To all intents and purposes it means a straight line.

Rigging screw: Fitting for attaching stays and shrouds to the chain plates and finally for adjusting the tension (similar to a fence strainer).

Running: To sail with the wind astern.

Running rigging: Lines used to hoist, control and trim the sails, halyards, sheets etc.

Sail track: Rail running up the mast into which the sail is fitted, usually by a series of nylon 'slides'.

Scuppers: Drainway around the edge of the deck but more popularly refers to the holes or slots in the toe rail or bulwarks which allow the water to run over the side.

Sea cock: Valve fitted to any pipe (engine cooling water, sink drain, toilet etc.) at the position where it passes through the boat's hull.

Self-tailing winches: Winches used for hauling the sheets and halyards of special construction which do not require a second person to hand the rope. This allows the user to both turn the winch and hand the sheet; i.e. only one person is required to work them instead of the customary two.

Shackle: 'U'-shaped piece of steel with a screw pin which connects across the top to make an enclosed fitting. They have numerous uses aboard, for instance in joining the head of a sail to its halyard.

Sheet: Rope attached to the sail for adjusting its angle to the wind; the foresail is controlled by foresheets, mainsail by mainsheets etc.

Shroud: Wire which supports the mast laterally.

Slat: A word to describe the noisy motion of a sail as it falls from side to side as the yacht rolls in light wind.

Speed log: Instrument which gives speed and distance. It does not take into account tide, current or wind influence.

Spinnaker: A voluminous sail, usually brightly patterned, used when running down wind.

Spreaders: Arms which protrude from the mast – usually about half height – over which the upper shrouds pass and thus provide additional stiffening.

Squall (or line squall):   Sudden increase or shift of wind direction as cold front passes.

Standing rigging: Wire ropes including stays and shrouds used to support the mast.

Staysail: A second headsail set between the mainsail and the jib.

Storm jib: Small sail of strong material and construction for use in bad weather.

Swell: Long waves which remain after the wind has gone or which have travelled many miles from the place of the storm.

Tack: See 'go about'.

Tri-sail: Small storm sail set in place of the mainsail.

VHF: Very High Frequency; close-range radio telephone band.

Wake: The trail of disturbed water astern which indicates the boat's path.

Warp: Rope used for mooring, anchoring etc.

Weather side: Side on which the wind is blowing.

Yankee: A jib or foresail with a high cut foot. In rough weather it does not catch water and additionally gives the crew an unobstructed view ahead. It is easier to handle than a genoa.